MY LIFE AS AN OB-GYN:

A Look Behind The Scenes

By: Douglas Edw

Foreword by: Robert ... ..., M.D., MSHA

MY LIFE AS AN OB-GYN: A LOOK BEHIND THE SCENES

Library of Congress Cataloging-in-Publication Data

Names: Heritage, Douglas Edwin, 1948- author.
Title: My life as an OB-GYN : a look behind the scenes / by Douglas Edwin
   Heritage, M.D.
Description: Ocala, Florida : Atlantic Publishing Group, Inc., [2016] |
   Includes index.
Identifiers: LCCN 2016040827| ISBN 9781620232606 (alk. paper) | ISBN
   162023260X (alk. paper)
Subjects: LCSH: Heritage, Douglas Edwin, 1948---Health. |
   Gynecologists--United States--Biography. | Obstetricians--United
   States--Biography.
Classification: LCC RG76.H47 A39 2016 | DDC 618.10092 [B] --dc23 LC record available at https://
lccn.loc.gov/2016040827

Printed in the United States

PROJECT MANAGER: Rebekah Sack • rsack@atlantic-pub.com
ASSISTANT EDITOR: Taylor Centers • gtcenters@gmail.com
INTERIOR LAYOUT: Antoinette D'Amore • addesign@videotron.ca
COVER DESIGN: Meg Buchner • meg@megbuchner.com
JACKET DESIGN: Janine Milstrey • j.milstrey@red-cape.de

Printed on Recycled Paper

Reduce. Reuse.
RECYCLE.

A decade ago, Atlantic Publishing signed the Green Press Initiative. These guidelines promote environmentally friendly practices, such as using recycled stock and vegetable-based inks, avoiding waste, choosing energy-efficient resources, and promoting a no-pulping policy. We now use 100-percent recycled stock on all our books. The results: in one year, switching to post-consumer recycled stock saved 24 mature trees, 5,000 gallons of water, the equivalent of the total energy used for one home in a year, and the equivalent of the greenhouse gases from one car driven for a year.

Over the years, we have adopted a number of dogs from rescues and shelters. First there was Bear and after he passed, Ginger and Scout. Now, we have Kira, another rescue. They have brought immense joy and love not just into our lives, but into the lives of all who met them.

We want you to know a portion of the profits of this book will be donated in Bear, Ginger and Scout's memory to local animal shelters, parks, conservation organizations, and other individuals and nonprofit organizations in need of assistance.

– Douglas & Sherri Brown,
President & Vice-President of Atlantic Publishing

Acknowledgements

I want to thank my wife, Katie, and daughter, Barbara, who were kind enough to read the earliest part of this book and encourage me to keep writing.

I am grateful to my friend Dennis Higgins from Yorkshire, England, also an author, for his insightful comments.

My appreciation goes out to Dr. Robert Fraker, medical school classmate, friend, and colleague, for taking time from his busy schedule to write a Foreword.

Most of all, I want to thank my editors, Rebekah Sack and Taylor Centers, without whose advice this book would not have been possible.

Dedication

This work is dedicated to my father,
Edwin Hargrove Heritage (1915-1957).

I hope he would be as proud of me
as I was of him.

Table of Contents

Foreword 11

Introduction 13

Part 1: Getting There 15

    Fader's... 17

    Growing Up... 29

    Don 33

    University of Maryland 41

    OCD Breakfast 47

    The Dining Hall Bomb 51

    Raiding the Naval Academy... 55

Saved by President Nixon 61

A Thanksgiving Holiday 65

Part 2: Medical School 71

MCV, Friends, and Romance 73

Human Dissection 79

The Laughing Skull 85

David Hume 89

Dr. Odlid 93

Bloody Nose 99

The Fan 103

Bob Medland 111

Horror in the Vending Room 117

Grace Street 123

Two Faces of Death 127

Prolapsed Cord 133

Psychiatry 137

First Pelvic Exam 143

First Delivery 147

The Surgical Rotation 151

Plastic Surgery 155

A Big Mistake 161

Part 3: Internship and Residency 165

Folie à Deux 167

First Operation 173

Labor and Delivery 179

First Caesarean Section 185

Bones 189

Hysterectomies Above and Below 193

Harry Berdann 199

Curse and Abuse 203

Board Certification 209

Part 4: Private Practice 213

Katie 215

Eclampsia 219

Infertility 223

Two Patients with Twins 229

French Girl 235

Shoulder Dystocia 239

Ovarian Cyst 245

Ectopic Pregnancy 249

Circumcision 255

Placental Abruption 259

Endometriosis 265

Abnormal PAP 273

German Girl 277

Mary Boyd 281

Time to Quit 289

Appendix A: Medical Terminology 293

Appendix B: Tobacconist Terms................................301

About the Author..303

Index 305

Foreword

I remain humbled by the invitation to pen a forward for Dr. Heritage's account of a successful medical practice in Virginia. Our experience in medicine will always be more than classes, tests, national board scores, matching success, residency training, board certification, and clinical practice. These are the facts listed on any resume we write; those that earned us a sheep-skin hung on the wall of our offices. His recall of the trials of absorbing the body of basic medical science, clinical skills, and the pressure of constant testing in medical school is colored with a personal touch that allows the story to be as unique as an oil painting on prominent view in our personal study.

These interpersonal interactions have more to do with who we are than all the credentials. My personal professional growth was supported, encouraged, and nurtured in face-to-face patient interactions. I cannot repay the influence of my professors and colleagues that showed me how to put knowledge into practice. This required errors, corrective action, and continued evaluations. If we had not had the opportunity to interact with someone who challenged us to grow by example, most of us would not be the doctors we are. When life can seem so difficult at times, the humor in being able to laugh at ourselves remains a cure for so many ills.

These colorful stories of a medical practice make for a light, easy read. It reminds me that we had much in common. It will have a place in my library, maybe next to the treasured yearbook with an infamous comic book character, Alfred E. Neuman, on the cover.

-Bob Fraker, MD, MSHA

Robert Turnley Fraker attended the Medical College of Virginia-Virginia Commonwealth University from 1971 to 1975 graduating as a Doctor of Medicine. After serving as a general medical officer on the USS California for a year, he completed a urology residency at the Naval Regional Medical Center Portsmouth Virginia from 1977 to 1981. He retired from military service in 1997. He currently practices medicine but is retired from full-time practice. Dr. Fraker married in 1979 to Kate Barnes Fraker, a veteran of the Navy and now retired nurse, mother of two sons and two grandchildren. They reside in North Chesterfield, VA.

Introduction

*I*t never occurred to me that taking a job in a tobacconist shop would result in becoming a Doctor of Medicine. It's strange how the direction of your life can hinge on the most trivial things. Your drive to work is delayed a few minutes because you forgot your briefcase, and you avoid a fatal car crash. You meet your future wife because she is getting coffee at the same shop you entered at a whim. You spend your spare change on a scratch-off ticket and win $10,000. In my case, my life was changed because I was blending pipe tobacco for a certain elderly gentleman.

Most women dread a visit to the gynecologist. Their most intimate anatomy will be exposed, peered at, and probed. Embarrassing subjects such as sexual dysfunction, menstrual problems, and sexually transmitted diseases may be discussed. That's a difficult conversation, whether the doctor is male or female.

The doctor knows all about the patient — how old she is, how many kids she has, how she spends her day, and so on. But what does the patient know about the doctor? Some information is available as a public record — where he or she attended medical school, whether he or she is board certified, how long he or she has been in practice — but medicine is only a part of a physician's life. Where did he grow up? Were her teen years like mine? Does he have a sense of humor? What is medical school like? Why a career as an obstetrician-gynecologist?

My name is Douglas Edwin Heritage. This book is, in my case, the answer to those questions. I graduated from Towson Senior High School, north of Baltimore, in 1967. I received a Bachelor's degree from The University of Maryland in 1971. From 1971 to 1975, I attended the Medical College of Virginia-Virginia Commonwealth University School of Medicine in Richmond, Virginia, where I graduated as a Doctor of Medicine. From 1975 through 1978, I was a Resident in Obstetrics and Gynecology at the Medical College of Virginia Hospitals. I entered private practice in 1978, was certified by the American Board of Obstetrics and Gynecology in 1980, and became a Fellow of the American College of Obstetricians and Gynecologists in 1981. I was in continuous solo private practice from 1979 until my retirement on January 1, 2014. Those are my credentials — all a matter of public record. Now, I will answer those other questions.

During those 47 years of school, residency, and practice, I have experienced a number of memorable events. They all involve friends, colleagues, or patients. Some stories are funny, some tragic, and some frankly unbelievable. All are true. I hope you will enjoy these recollections as much as many of my family and friends have over the years.

~ PART 1 ~

Getting There

Fader's

"Hey, Doug! Got a smoke?" It was 1966. *The Good, the Bad and the Ugly* was the hit film. "Hang on Sloopy" was my favorite song on the radio. Movie tickets were one dollar, and hamburgers were 50 cents. Almost everybody smoked. Kids started in elementary school by sneaking one or two of their parent's cigarettes to share with their buddies in the tree house. By middle school, we were regular smokers. Cigarettes were easily obtained from vending machines, and nobody thought twice about selling them to kids.

"Here you go." I gave Bill a Chesterfield. Bill was a curly-haired second generation Scotts-American (his father was named Angus). He and I had been best friends since middle school. We liked unfiltered cigarettes — Lucky Strikes, Pall Malls, Camels. Filtered cigarettes were for wimps.

"You know," he mused, "we can get American smokes anywhere. Think how cool it would be to smoke some kind of foreign cigarette. Something nobody else has."

"Good idea! I'll look into it."

Checking the yellow pages, I found a tobacconist in downtown Baltimore named Fader's. It was a third generation business built right after the great Baltimore fire of 1904, just up the street from Baltimore's notorious "Block," which was known for its striptease shows and dirty bookstores. The original store was still there on Baltimore Street. Bill and I took a bus downtown. Entering the fusty old shop, we were greeted by a little old lady, her full head of hair shining with blue rinse.

"Hello, boys," she said cordially. "Can I help you?"

"Yes, thank you, ma'am," I replied. "Do you have any foreign cigarettes?"

"I believe we do. I'm Mrs. Fader. I must say you boys look a mite young to be smoking."

Somewhat discomfited, Bill replied, "No ma'am. We're both 16."

"Well, in that case, I will see what I can find."

As she rummaged around behind the cluttered timeworn counter, I took the opportunity to look around the shop. The air was redolent with cigar smoke, pipe smoke, and the odor of old wood. One wall was completely covered in pipes. Several display cases exhibited smoking accessories such as humidors and pipe stands along with what appeared to be very expensive pipes of briar and meerschaum in hand-fitted cases. An antique mahogany blending bar, which could have come from a saloon, sported jars of various kinds of tobacco.

"Here we are boys," Mrs. Fader said, producing several tins of cigarettes. "These are Sarajevos, made in Yugoslavia. Would they do?"

"Oh yes ma'am. They look fine." Fine wasn't the right word. These cigarettes, from a foreign city we had never heard of, in their neat red tin boxes with a picture of minarets on the lid, weren't fine. They were beyond cool! We thanked her heartily and left for home. For several weeks, we sported our exotic smokes around school, no doubt making ourselves look like insufferable dorks.

So, I smoked cigarettes as a teenager, but I was really attracted to the romance of the pipe. Perhaps the suave, pipe-smoking Hugh Heffner of *Playboy* influenced me, or maybe it was to emulate urbane English clubmen sipping cognac amid clouds of Turkish tobacco. My thoughts kept returning to the smells and sights of that old downtown store. Blending different varieties of tobacco to provide a unique taste and aroma seemed to be, in a way, like chemistry.

I had always wanted to be a chemist. My dad had been a chemical engineer. When I was eight, he took me with him to work at Fairfield Chemical in Baltimore. At this time, he was a manager and worked from an office, but it was the laboratory I wanted to see. The first thing I noticed was the pungent and sweet smell. I would recognize this exotic perfume — a blend of esters, aldehydes, and ketones — years later when I took organic chemistry in college.

A complex of glassware covered multiple benches. On one, condensers dripped amber fluids into bulbous flasks. On another, a beaker was boiling over a Bunsen burner. I was thrilled! I knew immediately that someday, I would work in a place like this.

Dad led me down a narrow set of concrete steps to the chill lab basement. Lined up on metal racks, box after wire-enclosed box emitted creepy rustling sounds.

"Fairfield makes insecticides," Dad explained. "These are our test subjects."

The better killing of bugs was not my interest, but I was soon to find one.

When I was in middle school, I checked out a library book about the long history of world-changing drugs, such as digitalis, aspirin, and morphine. It explained who discovered them and how. I decided I wanted to be a part of that world. I would be a pharmaceutical chemist.

In 1966, Fader's opened a branch store in Towson. I couldn't wait to check it out. It was a five-minute walk from school. And Mrs. Fader was behind the counter!

"Hello, Mrs. Fader," I introduced myself. "I'm sure you don't remember me, but I met you in the downtown store some time ago. I was looking for foreign cigarettes."

"I'm afraid I don't remember, but I'm pleased you found our new store. Is it cigarettes you want?"

"Actually, no. I was thinking of taking up the pipe."

"That would be an excellent idea. I assume you want to start with a briar pipe — they are the best in many ways. And what about tobacco? Many of our gentlemen prefer something on the sweet side but there is a whole range of flavors."

"What do you suggest?" I replied.

Leading me to a wall covered with pipes of every size and shape, she began a detailed explanation. "The pipes at this end are the most economical. They start at $5 [about $35 in today's money] but don't have much of a grain. Briar pipes are priced according to the grain of the wood. Our most expensive are called straight grains. The grain is perfectly vertical all around. They start at $50."

"I believe I'll start with a $5 model," I replied.

"Of course! Now, what shape? As you can see, there is quite a variety. Straight stems, bent stems. Some believe a straight stem looks better on a younger face."

"I'll take one with a straight stem."

"Very good. Now let's fit you out with tobacco." At the blending bar, she filled my new pipe with small amounts of various house blends for me to try out before I settled on a four-ounce pouch to take home.

I must have spent well over an hour chatting with her and making my selections. Before I left, I tried out the only tobacconist joke I knew, originally a prank call kids made to tobacco shops. You must understand that Prince Albert is a commercial tobacco packaged in tins and usually sold in drugstores.

"Do you have Prince Albert in a can?" I asked.

"Oh no," she replied. "We let him out long ago!"

I haunted Fader's, trying various blends. My folks had no problem with my smoking in the house. My collection of pipes began to grow. I also read everything I could find about pipes and tobacco. During my junior year in high school, I started looking for a part-time job. I immediately thought of Fader's. The Towson store was run by Mrs. Fader and a single employee, a retired gentleman named Otts. Maybe they could use some extra help. I decided to ask.

"Mrs. Fader, is there any chance I could get a part-time job here? You know, just working on weekends."

"Well," she replied, "I would have to ask my son Bill. He does all the hiring. He'll be in the Towson store on Saturday. Why don't you come by and ask him?"

I made sure to visit the store the next Saturday. Bill Fader was a slim man in his late 30s, the business founder's grandson. His short-cut black hair was just starting to show streaks of gray. He always wore a white shirt and bow tie. I later discovered that his friendly, low-key manner made him a charismatic salesman.

"Mr. Fader, I'm looking for a part time job. Mrs. Fader said to discuss it with you." Desperate, I added, "I'll work for a dollar an hour!"

"My mother mentioned you to me," he replied. "Otts is here alone on Friday evenings, and the store is the busiest on Saturdays. We could use some help then. How about that?"

"Yes sir! That would be great!"

"And I think we can do better than a dollar an hour. Can you start next Friday?"

Fader's was open on Fridays until 9 p.m. and on Saturday from 9 to 5 p.m. Like everything else at that time, it was closed on Sunday. I started part time in the spring. I loved my new job. I always wore a sport coat and tie. I learned to talk with a pipe clenched in my teeth. We were expected to smoke in the store. Fader's own tobacco blends were free; we had to pay for exclusive tinned brands like Dunhill. When things were slow, I played chess with Otts, but I really enjoyed dealing with the customers. I tried to mimic Bill Fader's affable and knowledgeable manner. My favorite shopper was a wife or girlfriend who wanted their partner to quit cigarettes and take up the pipe. I showed them the least expensive briars to start while I explained the merits of those costing a little more, gradually working up the price scale. Rarely would they leave without a pipe, humidor, ashtray, pipe cleaners, and a goodly supply of tobacco. As well as my hourly wage, I earned a sliding commission on sales. Most of that money I plowed back into better and better pipes.

That summer, I was shifted back and forth from the Towson to the downtown store as needed. It was there that I made friends with another young clerk. Frank was a rotund fellow in his early 20s. We fell into a friendly rivalry, trying to outdo each other with better and finer (and more expensive!) pipes. When the store wasn't busy, Frank and I experimented at the blending bar. I concocted a number of medium-strength English blends, while he favored a stronger, heavier, Balkan style. Frank had an inexhaustible store of terrible punning jokes, as in "people that live in grass houses shouldn't stow thrones." Even today, I some-times pull out one of his old saws.

Mrs. Fader left promptly at 5 p.m. each Friday. "Remember boys," she always admonished us, "if someone comes in to rob the store, one of you must rush to the back, shut the safe, and spin the dial."

"Yes, ma'am!"

"Of course, Mrs. Fader!"

Once she was safely out the door, Frank laughed and said, "If a stick-up man comes in, I'll offer him a new pipe!"

"And I'll throw in a pouch of tobacco!" I added.

Dedication to our job went only so far.

As well as clerking, Bill Fader would sometimes order us to the dank and dusty basement to mix large quantities of house blends. We filled a cement mixer with bales of the required tobac-cos and sent it spinning. After packing the finished product, we loaded it onto an elevator. Huge gears were used to raise it up to the sidewalk overhead. On one occasion, Frank and I had packed the platform with a load to be sent to the Towson store. Out on the sidewalk, we tried again and again to raise the steel lift cover without success. Frank started to laugh.

"What's so funny?" I asked.

"We must look like Laurel and Hardy trying to do this," he chuckled. I could immediately see what he meant. Frank was 5 feet 8 inches and weighed 200 pounds; he was Hardy. I was 6 feet 2 inches and weighed 150 pounds; I was Laurel.

I was behind the blending bar at the Towson store one hot, summer day in July 1967 when a stout, elderly gentleman came in. He was dressed in a dark suit with a stiff, white shirt and tie. With his fringe of white hair, glasses, and a face creased with smile lines, he looked like someone's favorite uncle.

"Good afternoon, young man," he said. "I'm in need of my tobacco."

"Of course sir," I replied. "Are you a regular customer? If you are, we probably have your mixture on file."

"You do. I've been trading with Fader's for many years — probably more years than you have been alive. The name is Shackleford — Dr. Shackleford."

"Yes sir. Just a moment." I rummaged through the thick card index for his particular blend. It turned out to be one rich in Latakia, Perique, and Virginia Bright — a classic English style, which suited his appearance perfectly. I began to weigh out each component and dumped them in the mixing bowl.

"You seem quite young to be working here," he commented. "Is this going to be your career? Are you planning to be a tobacconist?"

"No sir, this is just my part time job — more of a hobby, really. I'm starting school at the University of Maryland in September."

"Are you now? And what do you plan to major in?"

"Chemistry. I want to be a pharmaceutical chemist."

"Do you? It just so happens that a good friend of mine, Dr. Paul Tallelay, is the chairman of the pharmaceutical department at Johns Hopkins Hospital. Would you like to meet him? If you want, I'll give him a call."

This was one of those moments when your future swings in the balance. I could have politely declined. He could have forgotten to make the call. But I didn't, and he actually called. My life changed.

"That's very kind of you, doctor. If it's not too much trouble, I would really like to meet him!"

"No trouble at all, my boy."

Two weeks later, I sat in Dr. Tallelay's office at Johns Hopkins. The furnishings were of luxurious mahogany, the shelves crammed with textbooks and bound journals. Dr. Tallelay was trim with silver hair.

"Dr. Shackleford tells me you're interested in pharmaceutical chemistry."

"Yes sir, very much so. That's why I'm planning to major in chemistry starting this fall."

"An undergraduate degree is a good start, but to do any significant research in the pharmaceutical field, you'll need a Ph.D."

"Yes sir, I know that. I'm prepared to go on for an advanced degree."

"Have you ever considered a degree in medicine?"

I never considered myself good at dealing with people. Despite my success as a salesman, I never made the connection. "No sir. I would rather work in a lab than practice medicine." I explained about the books I had read and my eagerness to work in the same field.

"But consider. An M.D. gives you so much more flexibility than a Ph.D. It broadens your opportunities. As a Doctor of Medicine, you could continue with chemistry as a pharmacologist. But if you decided you preferred medicine, you could practice or teach. As a professor, you could do both."

"Thank you sir. You've given me a lot to think about."

That September, I registered my major as pre-med.

Growing Up

The house was a mess when my parents bought it. It was a last resort. They settled on it because of its potential.

I was born in 1948 on the New Jersey shore. My father worked in Manhattan. He was transferred to Baltimore when I was six. For months, we lived in a hotel while my mom and dad went house hunting. They finally decided on one in Towson, just north of Baltimore City.

The previous owners had seriously neglected their property. And they had terrible taste. The walls were painted a dismal purple. The ceiling lights were filled with dead flies. The hardwood floors were black with ground-in grime. The sole bathtub was stained a hideous brown, as if a serial killer had used it to dissolve a body. My mother was especially offended by the rows of oyster shells bordering the front walk. She was picking them up as the movers took in our furniture. My dad spent months sanding the floors down to bare oak. He replaced the kitchen sinks and re-plumbed worn out pipes with new copper. Together, my mom and dad painted and wallpapered every room. Finally, we had a house to be proud of. Shortly after all the work was completed, my father died of a heart attack.

I walked to elementary, junior high, and high school. I got good grades. I loved to read — a passion I acquired from my mother. I started with *Reader's Digest*, and by fourth grade I was reading unedited Victorian ghost stories. I had a little "lab" in the basement, and in middle school I won two regional science fair awards. When a teacher asked a question, my hand was always the first to go up. The other kids teased me and called me "the teacher's pet." To make matters worse, I was lousy at sports. Recess, and later Phys Ed, were humiliating. I was always the first knocked out of the dodgeball court and the last one picked for the softball team. My feelings hurt, but I kept them to myself. Fortunately, I always had one or two similarly afflicted friends to pal around with.

I was in the accelerated program from third grade on. Unfortunately, the same classmates followed me from elementary to junior high school, along with their taunts and jibes. I couldn't shake the image of a dork. By the end of ninth grade, I had had enough. I desperately needed a new persona. Whatever it took, I was going to make a change in my life. I had no social skills. I needed someone to show me a new way.

I decided to approach the most popular girl in class. "Christie, I'm sick of being an outcast. I'm sick of being the nerd that nobody likes. What can I do to fit in?"

Christie Johansen had bobbed blonde hair and was cute in the American girl-next-door way. Everybody liked her. She never derided me like most of the "mean girls" in our class.

"Doug, you need to get some new friends."

"You are so right!" I had been in class with the same people for the past eight years.

"I know a lot of kids who go to Delaney Valley Middle," she went on. "They're gonna be at Towson Senior in the fall. How about if I introduce you around?"

"Gee, Christie! That would be great!"

"Sure! One other thing, though. Change your haircut!"

That summer, I let my crew cut, which was popular when I was 12, grow out. Christie brought several of her friends over to my house. They liked me. I liked them. Some illicit drinking may have been involved. I went on several double dates with Christie and her boyfriend. They were pretty tight, so I never asked her out myself. But I sure wanted to. By the start of my sophomore year, I was a new person.

Don

One of my new friends, Don Clemson, had been brought up to the strict standards of his father, a deacon in the Presbyterian Church. Tall and sporting his brown hair in a monk's cut — minus the tonsure — he was the poster child for "All-American Boy." He didn't smoke, drink, or play cards — things my friends and I loved. Naturally, we immediately set about to corrupt him.

Cards were the easy part. Bill and Lyle were my two best friends. We liked to play dealer's choice nickel and dime poker. Don was eager to join in. Smoking was a little harder. In those days, almost everybody smoked. Even middle school kids carried packs of Marlboros and Winstons openly in their breast pockets. Don started with cigarettes, and he soon advanced to cigars. From that point on, persuading him to drink a beer was only a short step. But as it turned out, he took it way too far.

We had started a poker game in my living room while my parents were away on a cruise. Besides Bill and Lyle, we had invited a new guy who drove up in his brand-new Chevell SS 396, its rumbling dual exhaust announcing his arrival. Don was late, so we started without him. We heard a knock on the front door.

"Must be Don."

Don seemed a little off balance and had a silly grin plastered on his face.

"Been drinking already?" I asked.

"Just a couple of beers. Where's the bathroom?" Off he went down the hall.

We played a few more hands, but time passed, and Don still hadn't come back to join the game.

"Where's Don?"

"I don't know. He got here at least 15 minutes ago. I'll go find him."

I pushed the bathroom door open and flicked on the light. He wasn't there. I heard a noise coming from the kitchen. Don had found my parents' liquor cabinet and was drinking bourbon straight from the bottle.

"Don! What the hell are you doing?"

"Just having a drink. Some problem with that?"

"Yeah, there's a big problem! I have to account to my folks for the whiskey, and you're drunk! Still want to play poker?"

"Nah, I need some fresh air."

Before I could stop him, he was out the door into the front yard.

"Is that Don howling out there?" He was making a tremendous racket.

"We gotta get him out of here! The neighbors are gonna call the cops!" The four of us rushed out to find Don staring at the moon.

"The moon makes dogs howl," he shouted. "Like this! Yaaah-woooo!"

Lights were coming on in the neighbors' houses. Forget the cops — it would be a disaster if they reported to my parents. "Let's just put him in the car and go!"

The only car big enough for all of us was New Guy's brand new SS Chevell. We dragged Don into the back seat and piled in.

"Where do we go?"

Thinking quickly, I said, "There's a golf course off Stevenson Lane." It was beside my elementary school. "We can take him there and walk him until he sobers up."

Off we went, the engine roaring as New Guy worked his way through the gears. The golf course was deserted, and no lights were on in the solitary house across the street. It seemed the ideal place to sober him up.

"I'll go first," I volunteered. "Come on, Don. Let's go for a walk."

"Am I home yet?"

"No, Don. It's just a place to walk. Come on." I grabbed his arm, and we walked about a hundred yards and turned around.

"Doug, you're my only friend. All the others hate me!" Don sobbed.

"You're wrong, Don. We're all your friends."

"No ... no ... you're my only friend."

Back at the car, I turned him over to Lyle. When he got back, it was Bill's turn.

"He says I'm his only friend," Lyle laughed.

"No, that would be me," I responded.

As Bill escorted him back, Don broke free and scrambled up a tree beside a rank-smelling creek, all the while letting out a mewing noise. The scene was getting weirder by the minute.

"Don, get out of the tree!"

"No, I'm a cat. Cats climb trees."

"Don, if you don't come down, we're going to leave you here!" We knew we wouldn't actually do that, but a threat was in order.

"Get me some milk. Cats love milk."

"Don, if I get you some milk, will you come down?"

"Sure!"

Leaving Bill and Lyle to watch over him, New Guy drove me home to fetch a glass of milk. We rushed back and offered up the milk to Don.

"OK, Don. Here's your milk. Now come on down like a good kitty." Starting down, he slipped and fell into the creek. We hauled him out, dripping and covered in slimy mud. By now, lights were flicking on in the house across the road.

"We gotta go!"

"I think I'm going to be sick," Don moaned.

"Well, hurry up and puke! Do it now!"

"He better not puke in my car," growled New Guy.

Don retched a bit but didn't throw up. "It's OK. I feel better now."

"Don, you're sure you're not going to puke?"

"Yeah, yeah, I'm fine."

As soon as we got him into the back seat, he vomited a full load of dinner, beer, whiskey, and milk all over himself and New Guy's car. The smell was revolting.

"Oh Jesus!" New Guy groaned.

"We'll clean it up later!" The front door of the house across the way began to open.

"Step on it!" New Guy floored the accelerator, leaving a good bit of his rear tires on the road. As we sped off, Don rolled down his window and screamed, "Help me! I'm being kidnapped!"

"Shut up, Don! Nobody's kidnapping you!" He continued to struggle.

"So, where to now?" From his tone, it was clear that New Guy was really pissed off. Who could blame him? All he had figured on that night was a cheap game of poker.

"Keep going. There's a shopping center up ahead. It's after midnight. By now, the parking lot will be deserted."

Arriving at the shopping center, dimly lit by yellow sodium light, Don — still convinced he was being kidnapped — threw open the car door and leapt out, snagging his toes on the doorsill and sprawling face-down on the blacktop.

"Son of a bitch! Just look at him!" Don had given up and now lay in a pitiful huddle, moaning, drenched, and covered in mud, vomit, and cinders.

"Guys," I said, "it's 2 a.m. We gotta take him home." Don was a good friend, but enough was enough.

"If his father catches him, he'll kill him," said Bill. He belonged to Don's church and was familiar with his strict parent's unforgiving ways.

"You got a better idea?" Nobody had a better idea. Headlights off, New Guy rolled his car to a quiet stop in front of Don's house. All the windows were dark.

"Don, can you get in without waking everybody up?"

"Yeah, I'll go in the back door," he slurred.

"Lyle. Bill. We better go with him."

We followed Don along the side of his house as he stumbled and knocked over several garbage cans. Crashing cymbals couldn't have been any louder. Not wanting to be seen, we waited at the corner, watching Don fumble at the back door.

The kitchen light came on.

We heard the door open.

A hand reached out and yanked Don off his feet.

The door slammed.

We didn't see Don again for quite a while.

University of Maryland

***

I entered the University of Maryland at College Park in the fall of 1967. The Vietnam War was at its hottest, and antiwar protest was just as hot. Hippies were on their way to San Francisco. The Doors had made it big time with "Light My Fire." Lyndon Johnson was president. *Bonnie and Clyde* was the hit movie that summer. Rock stations played a mix of soul and psychedelic. Mustangs and Camaros were the cars everybody wanted. I met my new girlfriend, a cute blonde named Dee, and together we indulged in a lot of night moves. The next year would see the national convulsion that followed the assassinations of Martin Luther King and Robert Kennedy. It was an interesting time to be 18 years old.

The U of M bordered Route 1 just a few miles from the Washington D.C. line. A cluster of brick high-rise dorms, eight stories tall, was located at the north end of the sprawling campus. That was where I lived. To the south were older cottage-like dormitories built in the '20s. There was a degree of rivalry between the high-rise and cottage residents. The high-rises had newer and better facilities; the cottages were quaint and closer to the town of College Park. "Temporary" clapboard shotgun classrooms lay on the southern border over a mile from my dorm. Erected during WWII, they were still in use. I often had classes there and consequently got a lot of exercise. The lecture halls, libraries, laboratories, administration buildings — everything that makes up a great university — were in the middle.

The town of College Park itself didn't have much to offer students: the college bookstore, a barbershop, a couple of sandwich shops. One of the two available watering holes — the Rendezvous Inn, commonly known as "the Vous" — was located there. The other, the Town Hall, was further north on Route 1. The drinking age for all alcoholic beverages was 21 in Maryland. A canny businessman had long ago realized the opportunity posed by lots of nearby underage college students by building a bar just on the city side of the Maryland/D.C. line. Beer was legal in Washington at age 18. Freshmen flocked to Ria's by the score.

Bill and I were rooming together in one of the high-rises.

Nick the Greek lived on the same floor. "Hey, Nick! Are you going into town tonight?" It was a typical Friday night in the dorm. "Can you give us a lift to Ria's?"

"I don't know," Nick replied, fingering his worry beads. "What's it worth to you?"

You could catch a bus to Ria's, but that wasted valuable drinking time. It was easier to hitch a ride with Nick. Freshmen couldn't have cars on campus, but Nick was an upperclassman. He had an old clunker, and for a few bucks, he would let us ride with him on his way to a Greek bar downtown. A gaping hole in the rusted-out floor provided an excellent view of the road passing by. Nick called it air conditioning.

"OK, OK; I'm going now," he snapped impatiently. "Get in or forget it."

Bill and Bob, a new friend from down the hall, joined us. We jumped in the back seat, trying to avoid the worst of the rust. Nick let us off at the D.C. line, and we strolled into Ria's. It wasn't much to speak of. The single room was crammed with as many tables and chairs as possible. The air was thick with cigarette smoke and the dank smell of spilled beer. A brightly-lit jukebox added a little color to the drab atmosphere. But a goodly-sized mug of draft beer went for a quarter. We picked a table and settled in for a night of drinking. As the night wore on, other friends joined us. The conversation was lively.

"So how do you like the Sgt. Pepper's album?"

"Lucy in the Sky with Diamonds" was playing on the jukebox.

"Big deal. The Beatles are just playing catch-up. Psychedelic is where the action is. Take Jefferson Airplane, for instance — that's where it's at. Grace Slick? She blows me away with that White Rabbit song!"

"I wish we could get some of those mushrooms she sings about! And 'a hookah smoking kummakir has given you the call!' What the hell is kummakir anyway?"

"Hey, did you hear? Patterson's old man gave him a GTO for his birthday!"

"GTO, GTO!" A little riff on the Beach Boys starts up around the table only to quickly fade away. None of us could sing.

"Yeah, Slick's cool. But you know, the Airplane's going down. Cream is where it's at. Nobody can play the guitar like Clapton!" And so the conversation went.

After five or six beers, we were feeling pretty mellow. We called for cigars. The waitress brought a box of nasty-looking cheroots from behind the bar. We all lit up. Somebody punched up "Gimme Some Lovin" on the juke.

"Hey, it's Daze's favorite song!" Daze, otherwise known as Michael Borman, was a big fan of soul and was famous in the dorm for his dance moves. A Jew, he had a black girlfriend. They visited Baltimore dance clubs on most weekends. According to legend, the other dancers would form a circle to watch them. A skinny Jew being applauded in a mostly black club by other black dancers was quite an accomplishment.

"Here's to Daze!" somebody shouted drunkenly.

At about eight beers, we called for pizza. By closing, I had put down 12. Bob and Bill, not to be outdone, had matched me beer for beer. "They're gonna kick us out," Bill slurred.

"Yeah, yeah," I replied. "Less see if we can get on the right bus this time!" I mumbled.

At this late hour, only two buses traveled north on Route 1. One went all the way to College Park, about five miles, the other turned off about half the way back. We always got on the wrong bus and had to walk the rest of the way. A bus approached. The door opened.

"Are you go'n back to the University of Maryland?" I asked the driver, doing my best to speak distinctly.

"Yes," he replied.

"Are you sure you're going all the way?"

"Yeah, yeah. Get on. I don't have all night."

We staggered on and fell into our seats. Success! We had finally gotten the right bus! Halfway up the road, the driver pulled over.

"Fellows, I'm really sorry. I usually drive the route you want, but tonight I'm filling in for a friend. I forgot that I have to turn off here."

So, as usual, we walked back to school.

OCD Breakfast

My dorm, Cambridge Hall, was an all-male dorm. In 1967, there was no such thing as co-ed living. It was an eight story brick building on the west side of a quadrangle. Facing to the east was the women's high-rise, and completing the square, two six-story men's dorms on the sides. The one-story dining hall occupied the center of the quad.

"Where's Dietrich? There's a Hearts game starting in the lounge, and they need a fourth."

"Are you kidding? It's 10 o'clock. Dietrich's asleep by now."

Rick Dietrich was a business school major, and, as such, could have been the poster child for obsessive-compulsive disorder. He always got up at dawn and went to breakfast as soon as the dining hall opened. Consequently, he was invariably in bed by 10.

I liked to sleep late and never went to breakfast. Dietrich's early rising somehow annoyed me. "What if Dietrich went down for breakfast and the dining hall was closed?" I mused.

"Yeah, but the dining hall opens at six and he always sets his alarm for 5:30," Daze countered.

"OK, but what if someone were to, say, set his clock ahead?

It was a December night. The sun wouldn't rise until seven. We snuck into Dietrich's room at midnight. He was fast asleep. We turned the hands on his old-fashioned wind-up alarm clock to read 5:25 and headed off to the communal bathroom. We were shaving and brushing our teeth when Dietrich came in a few minutes later.

"Hey, Rick," I said. "Off to breakfast as usual? It's pretty cold this morning. Be a good one for sleeping in."

"Better hurry!" Daze added. "I hear they got waffles and sausage this morning! You know that won't last long!"

"Why are you always up so early?" I asked as I combed my hair.

"I keep telling you guys," he replied tiredly. "I've got seven o'clock classes. Gotta eat first." I guess he was too sleepy to wonder why I was up at this hour.

He finished his morning chores. A few minutes later, he was waiting for the elevator dressed in a wool hat and winter coat. We watched with glee from the bathroom window as he pounded on the darkened and locked dining hall door. Ten minutes later he was back. Nobody could keep a straight face.

"Gee, Rick. Guess the dining hall's not open."

"Very funny … You guys are so very funny! It better not happen again!"

"I don't know, Rick. Maybe you should get an electric alarm clock!"

The Dining Hall Bomb

"The food here sucks!" Cresner was complaining as usual about the dining hall food. "We pay a lot of money and what do we get? Crap! We should do something about it."

"And just what might that be?" Bill replied sarcastically.

Cresner was the crazy man of the dorm. He fancied himself a barbarian and went around campus wearing a shaggy old coat that must have come from the back of a wild animal. His room was filled with swords and makeshift spears. He was the leader of a pack of like-minded Dungeons and Dragons fans who called themselves "The Golden Hoard." Though not an official member, I was accepted by the Hoard on a casual basis. I was hanging out in Cresner's room along with his then-roommate Bob. Bob and I later became good friends and roomed together our sophomore year.

"Have you ever heard of ammonium iodide?" Cresner asked rhetorically.

"What's that?"

"Iodine crystals soaked in ammonia. Nothing happens when they're wet. When they're dry, they explode under pressure, kind of like a cap. We could make some and spread them around the dining room."

"Cool!"

That night, we paid a visit to the chemistry lab. The university was more trusting in those days; the building was left unlocked so authorized students could work at night. We weren't authorized, but nobody confronted us when we walked in. It took only a few minutes to find a bottle of ammonia and one of iodine crystals.

"How do we spread them?" Cresner asked the next day at lunchtime.

"Let's all take a handful," I replied. We let the wet crystals dribble from our fingers as we went down the serving line. Seated at a table close by, we waited for them to dry. Soon enough: *snap, snap, snap!* came from under people's feet. Variations of "What the hell?" were shouted around the room as students did a little dance.

"That's great," Bob laughed. "But I've got an even better idea. How about a bomb?"

"That sounds kind of extreme, Bob. We don't want to hurt anybody."

"Not a big bomb, and not actually *in* the dining hall. We could put it on the roof after it's all closed up. Nobody gets hurt."

"So let's tie a bunch of cherry bombs together!"

"Nah, too ordinary. Somebody's always setting off firecrackers. We want something that will make a statement."

We were convinced. It just so happened that on arrival, each freshman was given a toiletries gift pack that included a half-sized can of Ban spray deodorant. "A Ban can will make a great casing. We fill it with sugar and some kind of oxidizer." From previous experiments, we knew that sugar and an oxidizer burned furiously. "We can get what we need from the chem lab."

"Yeah, but a can's too flimsy — it won't hold the explosion."

"It will if we wrap it with enough electrical tape!"

After another midnight visit to the chemistry building, we came back with several rolls of electrical tape, a bottle of oxidizer, some magnesium turnings, and magnesium dust. Blended together with sugar from the dining hall — it seemed only fitting that it should contribute — we stuffed the mixture into a Ban can wrapped with three rolls of tape. A fuse taken from a cherry bomb completed the assembly.

"So who's going to put it on the roof?"

"My idea. I'll do it!" Bob said with a grin.

It was a pitch black, weekday night at about 9 p.m. Yellow light gleaming from windows around the quad suggested that most people were in their rooms. As we watched from the seventh story windows, Bob scrambled onto the dining hall roof. He set our surprise down dead center and stuck a lit cigarette on the end of the fuse. From past experience, we knew it would take six minutes to burn down. Plenty of time for Bob to make his getaway.

Our expectations were greatly exceeded when the whole quad suddenly flashed an eye-blinding white accompanied by a thunderous *CRAAAACK!* like a lightning strike. A shower of flaming white-hot magnesium turnings soared 50 feet in the air. There was a moment of stunned silence; then, the first firecracker was thrown from an adjacent dorm window.

"Unbelievable!" we shouted as a riot started. Dozens more firecrackers followed the first. Guys streamed outside, shouting and whooping. On the porch below, a group of nude males gathered. Then, led by a leader brandishing a flaming broom, they proceeded to streak around the quad, making sure to pass in front of the girls' dorm.

It was incredibly satisfying.

Raiding the Naval Academy

"We play a basketball game against the Naval Academy tonight," Cresner noted, always looking for a chance to pull a prank. "Why don't we wrap Tecumseh in toilet paper?" Tecumseh is a statue and mascot standing in front of Bancroft Hall, the midshipmen's dorm.

"I can think of several reasons," I replied. "First off, we would have to do it at night, and the gates are closed at night, which means we'd have to break in somehow, and if we get caught, the midshipmen will beat the crap out of us. Not to mention the trouble we'd be in with the law and the university administration."

"Ah, don't be a wimp. Bob and Anderson and a couple of other guys already said they were up for it. You know it would be fun!"

I didn't agree, but they were right. I would be a wimp if I stayed behind. Against my better judgment, I was in. We dressed all in black with burnt cork smeared on our faces, and we pulled on black watch caps. The commando team was ready!

Dobbins, a junior, had agreed to drive us to Annapolis but wouldn't participate in the raid. He paused the car alongside a brick wall encircling the Naval Academy. "It's eight o'clock. I'll be here at midnight to pick you up. If you're not here — tough titty. You can find your own way home!"

He drove another few blocks and pulled over at a spot Cresner had already scouted out. A section of chain-link fence had come loose along the edge of the Academy grounds. The tidal smell of the Severn River greeted us as we slipped through the gap. Low-hanging clouds in the distance reflected stadium lights from below. Drums were beating. A far off crowd was roaring.

"What the hell is that?"

"It can't be a basketball rally. It's outside."

"Well, yeah. What was your first clue?"

"Hey, I just remembered. Navy is playing a big football game tomorrow against Clemson. That's a football rally!"

"That's just great! They're going to be expecting some kind of prank from the Clemson fans. The grounds are going to be crawling with mids on the lookout!"

"We're going to have to hide until it's over."

We slipped through the dark to a nearby gazebo. There was space underneath where we took shelter. The ground was damp and stunk of earth and mold.

"What time is it?"

"Nine."

"Sounds like the pep rally is dying down. Let's wait half an hour, then go for it."

"OK, but remember, Dobbins is leaving at 12."

"There's plenty of time," Cresner stated matter-of-factly.

Thirty minutes later: "Come on," urged our fearless leader. We crept out, groaning after crouching so long. It turned out that Cresner had only the most general idea where Bancroft Hall was located. Fortunately, we didn't encounter anyone as we aimlessly wandered about. Eventually, we came to a construction site.

"Look," Cresner crowed. "The steam tunnels!" Gigantic pipes exited into the open pit. "I bet they lead right to the quad and Tecumseh!"

Cresner was a steam tunnel rat. Once, we followed him through the tunnels at school and discovered an unused fallout shelter. The plundered survival crackers served as snacks for several days.

"At least nobody will see us," I said as we made our way into the pitch black opening. We went trudged through the inky darkness by flashlight. After a hundred yards or so, a manhole appeared eight feet overhead.

"I bet that opens onto the quad," Bob said. "Doug, get on my back. You're tall enough to raise the cover." Standing on Bob's back and gripping the rim, I was able to use my head to lift the cover a few inches. We were at the quad all right. Directly in front of me was the Tecumseh statue bathed in floodlight. Bancroft Hall was to the left. Ten feet ahead were two midshipmen staring at the face that had just popped out of the ground!

"Go, go go!" I shouted as I jumped down, letting the manhole cover slam closed. "They saw me!"

We raced pell-mell farther down the tunnel, away from our entry point. A patch of lighter darkness in the distance indicated an exit. We spilled out onto a mud-covered field, which was being cleared for construction.

"Who's there!" a bullhorn bellowed. Searchlights began to sweep the area. We flattened into the mud. I know I was scared. I'm sure my fellow commandos were, too. The horrible consequences of being caught flashed through my head.

"I don't know about you," I said to the others, "but I think we should forget about toilet-papering Tecumseh!"

"Yeah … right … good idea," the rest agreed.

The searchlights stayed on for about 10 minutes. It seemed like 10 hours. We could hear guards prowling around, shaking the bushes. Finally, the lights went off. We crept back in the general direction we had entered. We could hear a search party behind us. The edge of an excavation brought us to a stop. The pit was two stories deep, the bottom covered in a tangle of twisted, rusted rebar and broken glass. A single 12-inch plank spanned 20 feet to the other side. Without a pause, my friends ran across it. Now, I was never any good at gymnastics in high school, and I particularly hated the balance beam. But with the sound of pursuit spurring me on, I was across that plank like a Flying Wallenda!

In relative safety, we paused to catch our breath.

"What time is it?"

"11:30! Dobbins leaves in half an hour!"

"Which way is the road?"

"I think it's to the left."

"No, it's gotta be to the right!"

For the next 15 minutes, we groped around in the dark, afraid to use our flashlights. By dumb luck, we came upon a service road paralleling the highway. Faculty houses lined the inner side. On the outer was an eight-foot brick wall.

"I recognize this spot!" Cresner exclaimed. "Dobbins should be parked in the next block."

One by one, we boosted each other over. Bob and I were the last to go. Lights began to come on. Using his folded hands as a stirrup, I scrambled to the top and extended an arm to pull him over.

"We made it! There's Dobbins' car."

Back at the dorm, we stopped shaking and had some beers and a good laugh. A few weeks later, Cresner led a second commando raid with success.

I was invited along but declined.

Saved by President Nixon

1970. Rock music had mellowed out. Psychedelic was dead, and soul was in the doldrums. Groups like Three Dog Night and The Carpenters dominated radio. *M*A*S*H* was the No. 1 movie, its anti-war theme in perfect accord with the times. Promising to end the Vietnam War, Richard Nixon had been elected president the year before.

"In ziss class, you vill read und translate ze stories from your textbuuk. All class discussion vill be in Deutsch," the instructor informed us.

It was my first day in advanced German literature class. The pre-med program required four semesters of foreign language.

I had taken French in high school but hated it. German seemed a good alternative. Indeed, I had aced the first two semesters of German grammar and a third semester of introductory German literature. For the fourth, I could have opted for scientific German — as in "das carbon und die oxygen," but I had enjoyed the relatively easy basic German literature class. I chose advanced literature instead.

It was a huge mistake.

"You vill haff only two exams," the instructor continued, "ein midterm und ein final. For ze tests, you vill translate paragraphs from ze same stories."

It was the second semester of my junior year. I had crammed my schedule with 21 credit hours. My other courses included physics, embryology, quantitative analysis, and physiology, all of which required much more study time than I had allowed for. I tried to apply myself to German as well — at least at first. The stories were far in advance of those I had read in the introductory course, both in construction and vocabulary. Translating even a few paragraphs took hours. As the midterm exam approached, I hoped to just scrape by. I got an 87; the highest grade was a 93. The rest of the class of 15 failed.

"I am zo disappointed," the instructor lamented. "Zo many failures! I feel zat I have not been a good teacher. Zo I vill grade on und curve. Everybody gets zeven points." This gave the class leader a score of 100 and me a 94. Most of the rest got Ds instead of Fs.

As the semester progressed, I fell further and further behind. I didn't have time to translate any but one or two of the stories. I knew I was doomed by the time of the final exam. I would get an F. With my A on the midterm, I would finish with a C. Most people would be ecstatic to get a C in this class. But I wanted to get into medical school. Having a C would be a huge blot on my record.

Then, President Richard Nixon came to my rescue.

The Vietnam War was raging. Vietcong guerrillas were sheltering in Cambodia, formerly off-limits for American forces. In an effort to win the war, Nixon decided to bomb their refuges. Escalation was met with fury by antiwar protesters, of which there were many on campus. A riot started in College Park. Fires were lit on Route 1. Stores were vandalized; cars were overturned. As the mob became increasingly violent, the governor called in the National Guard. Tear gas was so thick that even a mile away, my eyes stung and watered. The university administration desperately wanted to restore order.

They met with a self-appointed committee of liberal students to work out a solution. As a condition to peace, the students demanded that final exams be cancelled (what this had to do with the Vietnam War and Cambodia escaped me at the time and still does). The administration agreed, but only partially. They argued that cancelling finals would not be fair to those who needed them to improve their grades. A compromise was reached. Final exams would be optional. You could elect to take the final or keep the grade you already had. I decided to skip the final and take an A.

The President of the United States had saved me. Later, even after Watergate and his resignation, I kept a soft spot in my heart for Richard Nixon.

A Thanksgiving Holiday

"Let's go for a ride and stop at some lamp stores on the way!" my aunt Connie announced cheerfully. I knew that "lamp stores" was a euphemism for "roadhouses." It was the day after Thanksgiving, and I had just turned 21 in September. "Roadhouses" sounded fine to me.

Connie was my mother's younger sister, one of 11 children. Born in Raleigh, she spoke with a strong North Carolina accent. She and her husband, Joe, a first-generation child of German parents, were my favorite relatives. Connie had curly blonde hair and the florid face of a chronic boozer. Joe's face would have been the same color, but years of pumping gas out in the sun had turned it the color of a well-used saddle. He ran a combination gas station-restaurant-souvenir shop on a highway paralleling the Delaware River. Located in the Pocono Mountains, it was about 10 minutes from the city of Easton, Pennsylvania.

Connie and Joe were both flat-out alcoholics. A case of Seagram's VO whiskey was delivered every week by standing order. Connie kept a bottle under the kitchen sink, and Joe kept a bottle under the store counter. First thing in the morning, they would start to take nips. At night, they drank together. But by and large, they were happy drunks and were always fun to be around. They had two children. Joanne, the older, was three years younger than me. Her brother, Joey, had been our nemesis when we played together as children.

For many years, my mother, my stepfather David, and I spent every Thanksgiving holiday with Connie and Joe. On Thanksgiving Day, we always attended the local football game between Easton High School and their long-standing rivals from across the river in New Jersey. The games were invariably intense, and emotions ran high. At one game I attended, there were three heart attacks in the stands, and one of the referees collapsed on the field with a coronary occlusion. On this particular Thanksgiving, my step-grandfather was staying at Connie's house. His last name was Blackwell, but everybody called him Blackie. A skinny bald man with a gray mustache, he was still spry in his 70s. He too spoke with a thick North Carolina accent.

"Everybody in the car," ordered my cousin Joanne. She was 18 that year, and her brother was 14. We crammed into Joe's Buick, a huge barge of a car with bench seats fore and aft. Joe drove with Connie, my mom, and David in the front seat. Blackie was in the back along with Joanne, Joey, and me. Off we went across the river to New Jersey.

"Stop here, Joe," Connie commanded. We hadn't been gone more than 30 minutes.

"OK, time to look at some lamps," Joe responded as he pulled into a roadhouse parking lot. We piled out and made our way into the comfortably dim pub. I took a seat at the bar along with Blackie, Connie, and Joe. My mom hardly ever drank. She and David sat at a table with the kids and ordered soft drinks. Blackie, Connie, and Joe ordered shots of VO whiskey.

"I'll have a shot of VO, too," I told the bartender. I figured I was an adult now and would drink like one. After a couple of shots, everybody squeezed back into the car, and off we went in search of the next watering hole. This went on all afternoon as I tried to match drink for drink with the old soakers. By sundown, I was feeling a little woozy.

"Joe, we need to stop for dinner," Connie said without any trace of a slur.

"Let's go to the Manhattan," he replied.

Joe's uncle owned the Manhattan, a nightclub and restaurant in Easton. Connie and Joe were well known there. Joe parked in a garage around the corner. We found a table big enough for eight and, of course, ordered drinks before dinner. When our meals were finished, we had after-dinner drinks.

"Joe, it's time to go," my mom spoke up.

"I'll get the car and bring it around," he replied. Off he went. We waited. No sign of Joe or the car. "I'll go get him," said Blackie. Off he went. We waited. No sign of Joe, Blackie, or the car.

"I guess I'll have to find them," Connie complained.

Off she went. We waited. No sign of Joe, Blackie, Connie, or the car.

"Doug, why don't you see what's going on," said my thoroughly exasperated mother. Off I went.

Somewhat unsteadily, I walked around to the garage. Connie and Joe were in the toll keeper's little glassed-in booth sharing drinks with him. "Guys, *guys!* Everybody's waiting for you. We need to get the car and go!"

"What's the hurry? Come on in and have a drink!"

That's where my mother, David, and my cousins found me when they gave up and, at last, made their way to the garage. My mom wasn't very happy, but at that point, I didn't care. They declined the offer of a drink, and we finally started home. Joe broke every speed limit on the winding, twisting road back, a rock face on one side of the highway, and the river on the other. There were no guardrails. I thought my mother would have a stroke. But eventually, we got back without incident.

"What we need are some martinis," said Joe — or was it Connie?

"Excellent idea!" I replied enthusiastically. But before the martinis were ready, it dawned on us that something wasn't right.

"Oh my God, where's Daddy!" shrieked Connie. "We left him behind!"

We were milling in confusion when there came a knock on the door. A strange man stood there.

"Does that old man in the back of my car belong to you?" he laughed.

Yes, he did. Blackie had gotten into the wrong car and had fallen asleep. As David and I carried him down the stairs to his bed, he kept grabbing the handrail and ranting, "I'll never forgive you for this! I'll never forgive you for this!"

It was the best Thanksgiving ever.

~ PART 2 ~

Medical School

MCV, Friends, and Romance

*D*uring my first year at MCV (the Medical College of Virginia-Virginia Commonwealth University), I lived in the men's dorm. The high rise women's dormitory, which housed nursing and female graduate students, was adjacent to the men's dorm. Guys and girls shared meals at the centrally located dining hall. It was an ideal arrangement for a bunch of horny young people.

It was the fall of 1971. Muscle cars were hot. The Plymouth Barracuda had just been released. Dirty Harry made his first appearance in movie theaters. The airwaves were full of "American Pie" and "A Horse with No Name," which featured the most grammatically incorrect lyric ever: "'Cause there ain't no one for to give you no pain."

"Hey, Doug! We're going to dinner," Ed announced. He and his roommate, Bob, had the dorm room next door to me. We had met just hours earlier. "Want to come with us?"

"Sure!" I was a little homesick. The thought of dinner by myself was too grim to bear. After passing through the cafeteria line, we set our trays down at a large table and were soon joined by other medical and nursing students.

"So, you must be in nursing," I said to an attractive, thin young woman with straight brown hair.

"So, you must be a male chauvinist!" she replied with a grin. "My name is Wendy. I'm a first year med student. You must be in nursing."

"No, I'm a med student too," I responded with chagrin. "Sorry about my mistake."

"That's OK. I think there are only three of four other females in our class."

I looked the table over as Bob and Ed introduced themselves. A cute girl with short blonde hair sat across from me. She was from Wilson, North Carolina. I loved to flirt with her, always addressing her as "Wilson." Another girl, this one with deep, brown eyes and long, brunette hair to match, caught my eye. Sensing my appraising look, she turned and said, "Hi, I'm Deborah, but call me Debbie."

"Are you a medical student, too?" I asked. I didn't want to put a foot in my mouth for a second time in one evening.

"No, I'm in the postgraduate program for genetics."

It turned out that Ed, Bob, Wendy, Debbie, and I would form a close-knit group. Debbie was to take on a special significance.

My grandparents had lived in Richmond. I was familiar with the town from many visits. I had heard about MCV since my teens. My aunt, Elizabeth Heritage, lived there still. She was a nurse at the McGuire Veterans hospital and during my summer vacation visits introduced me to some of the doctors there. They all held joint privileges with MCV. The Medical College of Virginia is rich in history. It started as a division of Hampden-Sydney College in 1837 and was the only medical school in the Confederacy, graduating a class during each of the Civil War years. Stonewall Jackson's personal physician, Dr. Hunter McGuire, joined MCV after the war in 1865 as Chief of Surgery and was elected president of the American Medical Association. His statue stands on the grounds of the State Capitol. The Medical College of Virginia became an independent institution in 1854. In 1968, it joined the Richmond Professional Institute to form the Medical College of Virginia-Virginia Commonwealth University School of Medicine.

In 1971, the Medical School of Virginia (MCV) campus consisted of four separate hospitals in addition to clinics, a library, an auditorium named "The Egyptian Building," and Sanger Hall, all clustered around Marshall and Broad Street deep in downtown Richmond.

The West Hospital, a cruciform brick building of 18 stories, was built on the corner of 12th and Broad Street in 1939. It was a facility used largely by Medicine, Surgery, and OB-GYN. The main operating rooms, private patient labor and delivery, and facilities for internal medicine patients were located here, as was the radiology department and the main emergency room. Four elevators, one in each wing, ran continuously.

The St. Philips Hospital, better known and referred to as the East Hospital, was completed in 1920. A six-story brick building, it was originally the hospital for African-American patients during the Jim Crow era. In my time, it was the hospital for staff patients — those under the care of the resident staff. The OBG emergency room was on the first floor. Labor and delivery rooms were on the second floor, but there was no Caesarean section room — the importance of this will become apparent in the later story, "Prolapsed Cord." Postpartum care was on the third floor. It was an old-fashioned ward with rows of chipped, white, pipe-frame beds separated only by curtains.

The Ennion G. Williams, or North Hospital, was built in 1956 as a new facility for African-American patients. In my time, it contained the pediatric unit and operating rooms used for gynecologic procedures.

The Egyptian Building, a National Historic Landmark, was built in 1845. Resembling an Egyptian temple, it mainly served as a lecture hall. Sanger Hall was the Medical Education Building. Facing Marshall Street, it provided the teaching facilities for students and clinical faculty, who had their offices and laboratories there. The dean of the School of Medicine occupied the first floor.

My walk to Sanger Hall took only a few minutes along pleasant, tree-shaded 12th Street, past the college bookstore and the White House of the Confederacy — Jefferson Davis' home during the Civil War. Richmond had been, of course, the Capital of the Confederacy and was a city of monuments. Practically every major street sported a general's statue. I probably would have sided with the Union had I been born in 1848 rather than 1948, but I felt at home. All my family was from North Carolina. My ancestors fought for the South during the War of Northern Aggression.

Another med student, Bob Fraker, lived locally with his parents. He gave a party at their house early in the semester. Only a few of us had cars, so I rode in his backseat with Debbie. Without any preamble, we started making out like fury. I don't remember much about Bob's party, probably because Debbie and I spent the whole night making out on the couch. I asked her out on a date the next week.

Santana was performing at the Richmond Colosseum, a five-minute walk from the dorms. We paid attention to the music while the group performed their hit, "Black Magic Woman," but we ignored the rest of the concert to focus on each other.

A medical degree required four years of school. At MCV, the first year addressed the function and structure of the healthy human body. I sat through classroom lectures about anatomy and physiology, my mind bouncing from the muscular system to Debbie's deep brown eyes, from the circulatory system to her soft brunette waves, from the nervous system to her easy-going personality, from the digestive system to the way I felt when she was around, from the endocrine system to what I was going to do about it all. Other lectures reviewed biochemistry and pharmacology, and while I was fully engrossed in my studies, all I really cared about was Debbie.

Debbie was pretty, smart, and talented. We both enjoyed books, music, and film. It became a romance in short order. We got together every day, almost to my detriment. I spent so much time with her that I neglected my studies. It couldn't have been at a worse time, because the subject at that time was Neuroanatomy, probably the most difficult course I have ever taken. With the exam looming, I realized I was hopelessly behind. It took an entire day locked away with my books and notes — as well as several pots of coffee — to catch up.

Thank God the grading at MCV was pass/fail.

I passed.

We were engaged before the first year was over.

Human Dissection

- ONE YEAR EARLIER -

"Here's the secret door they used to bring in bodies from the graveyard," announced the upperclassman who was showing me around the facilities. He continued, "In the 1800s, there were never enough legally available bodies for dissection, so the students sometimes had to make use of the resurrection men."

I was visiting a well-known East Coast medical school. We were standing in the pit of the lecture hall, facing tiers of hard, wooden benches rising to the ceiling. It was my senior year at the University of Maryland. I was visiting medical schools where I had been accepted.

"And in the hall, as you probably saw when you came in, we have the collection of the famous Scottish anatomist, William Hunter."

I had, in fact, passed by this exhibit when I arrived. It seemed better suited to a chamber of horrors than a medical school. Glass cases ran the length of the gloomy corridor, each exhibiting a mummified human head, which had been split down the center, the veins and arteries injected with faded colored wax. The cases looked like they hadn't been dusted since Truman was president.

"And here," he continued proudly as we rounded a corner, "is the gross anatomy lab."

Yellowed porcelain slabs filled the room. A gutter down each side allowed cadaver fluids to drain.

"So, what do you think?" he continued brightly.

"Well, it's certainly interesting from a historical point of view. Thanks for showing me around." I wondered how anyone could stand such a depressing environment, especially in light of the school I had visited the week before — MCV.

"This is the lecture hall for first year students."

I was being shown around Sanger Hall, the medical education and administration building. The brightly lit auditorium resembled a movie theater with rows of comfortable-looking padded seats.

"A lot of the professors use the audiovisual system," he continued. "There's a hookup in the library where you can watch tapes of the lectures. Now, let's take a look at the anatomy lab."

We took the elevator to the eleventh floor and exited onto a foyer. One wall held lockers for surgical scrubs, the other a set of double doors leading to the work area. It was huge. The outer wall was floor to ceiling picture windows providing a spectacular view of downtown Richmond. The airy space was filled with coffin-sized stainless steel tanks, their contents tastefully concealed by folding lids. A TV monitor was mounted at the foot of each tank to view videotapes. The other half of the room featured jars with specimens in formalin, anatomic models, and a number of waist-high shelves. "This is where they set up the practical exams," I was told.

There was no comparison. It was MCV for me.

-1971-

The first six weeks of school were devoted to a review of basic science — biochemistry and physiology. Having already taken those courses at Maryland, I did well without too much effort. I was impatiently looking forward to Gross Anatomy. Human dissection would be the first real step in my medical education. I had read all I could about it. What would the real thing be like?

"You have all had experience with dissection — a frog or fetal pig, perhaps," Dr. Slidell, the head of the Gross Anatomy department, informed our class during his introductory lecture. He had a slight Swedish accent. "A man or woman is a different matter altogether. You will have to take your dissections to a new level. You must learn the structure of every bone, muscle, nerve, and organ of the human body. You will be expected to identify them during practical exams and describe their function. This will require a great deal of memorization, but I know you are all capable of it. Otherwise, you would not have been selected to attend this school." Immediately after this forbidding introduction, we crammed into the elevator for the eleventh floor.

Like my classmates, I put a surgical gown on over my street clothes before entering the lab. I soon found out that, despite the gowns, the unique odor of the anatomy lab — a distinctive inter-mingling of formaldehyde with a whiff of decay — permeated our clothes. You could always identify a first-year medical stu-dent on the elevator.

Four students were assigned to each cadaver. My partner Ray and I were on one side and two classmates were on the other. My pal Wendy and three others had the neighboring tank.

"What do you think we got?" Ray wondered.

"I guess it's the luck of the draw. Whatever it is, I hope it's thin."

Dissection would be a lot harder with a fat specimen.

Everybody waited nervously for the order to start. "Open up," Dr. Slidell announced. We flipped back the lid. The cadaver slowly rose out of a dark pool of embalming fluid as I turned a crank at the base of the tank. "Thank God!" Ray exclaimed. Ours was a thin old man, balding, with a gray beard. Around the room, our other classmates were inspecting their specimens with varying degrees of satisfaction.

"What's the problem?" asked a student at the vat beside us. Another was laboring over the crank. "Is it stuck?"

"No, it's turning, but it's hard as hell!" Ever so slowly, their cadaver rose from the depths. It was an enormous fat woman who must have weighed at least 300 pounds.

"Oh no!" the four cried in unison.

I could feel their pain. According to the syllabus, dissection started with the muscles of the back. It took all four of them to turn over their beached whale. With a touch of *schadenfreude*, I watched as they made their first incision. A putrid red liquid began to ooze out.

"Oh, God! What's that? That's not embalming fluid!"

"No, that's blood! Dr. Slidell, over here please!" Wendy cried out. The professor ambled over to see what the commotion was about. He took one look, and in his lilting Swedish accent said, "Oh, by golly, we will have to get you another one! It is very difficult to fully embalm a body of that size."

"Thank you, thank you!" the four responded.

There was never enough class time to complete the required work. Following the textbook, we had to tease out each individual muscle, nerve, and organ. During practical exams, we filed from station to station where a bit of tissue was set up with the following questions:

1. "What is it?"
2. "What does it do?"
3. "What innervates it?"

Illustrations and models were a big help, of course, but many hours of hands-on work and still more hours of tedious memorization were needed if you expected a passing grade. Accordingly, the anatomy lab was left open at night so we could put in extra time.

"What time is it, Ray?" I asked. It was Friday night. We had been anatomizing since dinner. "It's 8:50," he replied, checking his watch.

"Turn on the TV. 'Night Gallery' comes on at nine."

The televisions could play broadcasts as well as videotapes. Rod Serling's macabre weekly show was a class favorite. No one considered it strange to watch a horror show in a room full of dead bodies. We somehow disassociated our activity from the fact that these specimens had once been living human beings. We never gave our cadaver a name. He was simply a project — work to be completed and facts to be memorized. I often studied his receding hairline and trim beard, and I wondered: Who was this? Was he a homeless derelict without any relative to claim him when he died? Or was he a professor who nobly donated his body to science?

We would never know.

The Laughing Skull

"Do you have any notes from the lipid lecture?" Ed asked. He roomed next door with Bob.

"Yeah, for what they're worth. Did you fall asleep in class again?" I replied.

"Sure, like you stayed awake for an hour of Larry Lipid!"

Larry Lipid (not his real name) was the professor who had the dubious job of lecturing the first-year class on lipids. These fatty molecules are vital to life; without them, cells couldn't exist. But the professor's speaking style would put a methamphetamine addict to sleep. To make things worse, he looked and sounded like Gomer Pyle.

"You know what really annoys me," Ed continued, "is the way he starts each class with some lame joke. Then, he's disappointed if he doesn't get a big laugh!" To emphasize his point, Ed shook a little orange bag he had been fiddling with. "Ha, Ha, Ha!" loudly sounded from it.

"What's that?" I asked, mildly curious.

"It's just a toy my sister gave me. You shake it, and it laughs."

"You know, that gives me an idea. A great idea!"

One of the hardest parts of the gross anatomy practical exams dealt with the 12 so-called cranial nerves that exited the skull — the Olfactory, Optic, Oculomotor, Trochlear, Trigeminal, Abducens, Facial, Acoustic, Glossopharyngeal, Vagus, Spinal Accessory, and Hypoglossal nerves. We used a mnemonic device to memorize them: "On old Olympus' towering tops a Finn and German viewed some hops."

During a practical exam, we were required to identify each nerve, its exit point, and its function. These exit points, or foramen, can only be seen from inside the skull. Skulls, which had been opened, were available for study in the anatomy lab, but couldn't be checked out. I purchased one from a medical supply house to review when back at the dorm.

"Let me see that bag." It contained a plastic box about the size of a pack of cards. Inside were batteries, a speaker, and some simple electronics. "Look," I went on, "we can take the batteries out and hook a wire to the terminals. We put the box in my skull and take it to the lecture hall. We run the wire a couple of rows under the seats. You touch the wire to the batteries, and the skull laughs."

"Outstanding!" Ed exclaimed.

We arrived before class started the next morning. We put the skull on the lectern — what could be more natural than a skull on a desk in a medical school? — and ran the wire under the seats to the fourth row. The class filled up. Larry Lipid arrived.

"Well class, today's topic reminds me of a joke I heard…"

We touched the wire to the battery. "Bwahh ha ha ha" went the skull. Dr. Lipid's eyes bugged out as he jumped back. Staring intensely at the skull, he exclaimed, "Gee, I never… "

"Bwahh ha ha ha" went the skull. We didn't want to be obnoxious, so we didn't make the skull laugh again. Larry Lipid took things in the spirit they were intended, but at every pause in his lecture, he would glance apprehensively at his tormentor.

David Hume

"As you know, the liver is responsible for metabolizing and excreting the toxic products of metabolism." Dr. David Hume was lecturing to the first year medical class. "It is ordinarily quite efficient at this task, as many of you may know, having consumed large quantities of alcohol last weekend." Polite laughter. "But when the liver is damaged, say by disease or that same alcohol, it loses its ability to rid the body of toxins. With sufficient damage, the ultimate outcome is death."

David Hume was a world-famous pioneer in transplant surgery. He helped perform the first successful kidney transplant at Peter Bent Brigham Hospital in Boston. MCV was fortunate to acquire him as Chief of Surgery in 1956. Of medium height with a square jaw and close-cropped graying hair, I was immediately taken by his piercing gaze, which seemed to fix on each of us as it swept the classroom.

Much later in life, I read the following account of him by his colleague Thomas Starzl in his book about the history of organ transplantation, *The Puzzle People*: "Hume always reminded me of a human buzz saw, constantly advancing but with such precision and beauty of motion that it was a masochistic thrill to realize that the cutting pathway was directed straight to you. He had the whitest teeth I have ever seen, which were often displayed because he laughed at the slightest provocation, whether sad or happy."

It seemed like Dr. Hume was directing his lecture straight at me. He continued: "It would be ideal if we could transplant a healthy liver into these terminal patients. As you know, there has been some early successes with heart transplants and many successful results with kidney transplants. Sadly, all attempts at liver transplantation in animals have failed to date. But what if there was a machine that could cleanse the patients' blood, similar to the use of renal dialysis for kidney failure? Unfortunately, there is no such machine. However, it may be possible to borrow a liver temporarily."

At this point, the lights dimmed, and a silent black and white film started. A skeletal, bearded, comatose patient lay on a gurney. Tubing exited his groin and led out of the field of view.

"This patient is suffering from terminal alcoholic cirrhosis of the liver," Dr. Hume continued. "He has been in a coma for over 24 hours. If nothing is done, he will die."

The camera panned to the right, following the tubes that led to a baboon strapped to a gurney two feet away. "It so happens that a baboon can live for several hours after its blood has been completely exchanged with human blood. That has been done here to allow the baboon's liver to clear the toxins from the patient. The patient's arteries are now pumping blood to the baboon's venous system, the baboon's arteries returning cleansed blood to the patient."

The auditorium was dead silent, the only sound the whirring of the 16 millimeter projector. The patient's eyelids began to flutter and slowly open. He stared into space for a moment, no doubt wondering where he was. Then, he turned his head toward the baboon. The baboon turned its head to face the man and bared its fangs in a silent snarl. The film came to an abrupt end. I wondered if the patient — whose last memory was probably of a filthy alley and a cheap bottle of wine — believed he had died and gone to hell.

"As you can see," Dr. Hume continued, "The experiment was a success, though a temporary one. Hopefully, we will be successful with a human liver transplant in the near future. Are there any questions?"

The podium was mobbed, so I waited outside the auditorium on the off chance of meeting him at the elevator. I knew that he was a very busy man with a tight schedule, but I hoped he might spare me a moment. The elevator doors opened as he exited the classroom.

"Excuse me, Dr. Hume," I said. "If you have a moment, I have a question."

He ignored the waiting elevator and fixed me with his gaze. "Of course! Did you like the lecture?"

I have forgotten what my question was; I'm not sure I even heard his answer. For that moment, I was the only concern of this charismatic man.

But as great a man as he was, David Hume suffered from a malady affecting many physicians: ego and overconfidence. Doctors are used to giving orders and having them obeyed without question. With the marvelous power to heal and bend nature to their will, they often come to believe they can overcome any obstacle.

Dr. Hume piloted his own small plane. Shortly after delivering his lecture to my class, he flew it to a meeting in California. After landing, it seemed that his plane needed some work that would take a few days to complete. With his busy schedule, he couldn't afford to wait and decided to return to Richmond by commercial aviation. The repairs completed, he flew back to pick up his plane. The weather was unfavorable and visibility poor. He was advised to delay another day before returning to Richmond. His schedule wouldn't allow it. He took off anyway and flew into the side of a mountain.

It was the only time in my life that I had been face to face with a truly great man.

Dr. Odlid

"So, what's with your roommate?" Three or four of my dorm mates were gathered in Bob's room to celebrate completing our first exam. Grades would be mailed to us within a few days. "He looks like he's ready to jump out of his skin."

"You know Herb's backstory, don't you?" I replied.

"Yeah, kinda. A lot of doctors in the family, right?"

"To say the least." I helped myself to another beer. Jethro Tull was on the stereo. "His father is a doctor — so are his uncle and cousins. His younger brother skipped a few grades. He's already finished med school and is an OBG resident here at MCV. Herb brags about it all the time. Says they might get in the *Guinness Book of World Records* for the most doctors in a family."

"OK, that explains the nerves."

"Sure. He has to be a success or else he lets his whole family down. He sure has been cracking the books; didn't even take a night off for the party last week."

"I want a passing grade too, but nothing would have made me miss that social with the nursing students' dorm!" Bob remarked. "A lot of those girls are hot!"

"Anyway, he gave it a pass. Gimme another beer, *por favor*." I was feeling pretty good by now. "Grades should be in our mailboxes any day."

The dorm lobby sported a wall of post office style individual mailboxes. My evil twin suddenly sprang to life. "That gives me an idea," I continued. "What if we made a phony grade card for Herb and slipped it into his mailbox? We don't have to know the combination — it'll slide under the door."

"Yeah, but the grading is pass/fail. We can't fail the guy. He'd have a heart attack."

"You're right. It can't be a fail, and a pass is no good. It has to be something else. Wait! How about see doctor so-and-so to explain discrepancy?"

"That's great! Discrepancy could mean anything! Let's use the dean's name for the doctor."

By now I was in high gear. "No, he'll go right to the dean and see it's a joke. I've got it — how about 'see Dr. Odlid to explain discrepancy?'"

"Who's Dr. Odlid?" Ed asked. "I never heard of him."

"I can hardly believe you made it into medical school. Try spelling it backwards."

"D ... i ...l .... Got it. Perfect!"

We used a typewriter and an index card to make the following:

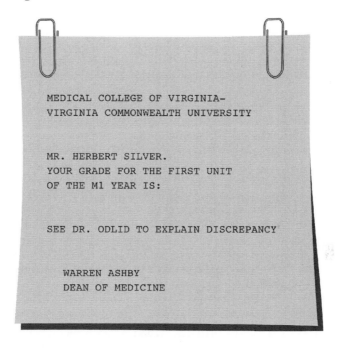

```
MEDICAL COLLEGE OF VIRGINIA-
VIRGINIA COMMONWEALTH UNIVERSITY


MR. HERBERT SILVER.
YOUR GRADE FOR THE FIRST UNIT
OF THE M1 YEAR IS:



SEE DR. ODLID TO EXPLAIN DISCREPANCY


    WARREN ASHBY
    DEAN OF MEDICINE
```

We also made fake grade cards for ourselves and slipped them into the mailboxes that night. The next morning, the other conspirators and I made sure to go to breakfast with Herb. On the way, we stopped by our mailboxes.

"Hey, the grades are out! All right! I passed!"

"Yeah, I did too!"

"What the hell is this?" Herb exclaimed, staring at his card in horror.

"What's the matter, Herb?" I asked helpfully.

"Explain discrepancy! What's that supposed to mean?"

"Gee, Herb, I don't know. Must be some problem with your exam. You better see this Dr. Odlid and straighten things out."

"Damn right I will!!" He was out the door and off to the administration building before the rest of us broke down in laughter. An hour later, he was back and not in a good mood.

"So, what's it all about?" I inquired with a straight face.

"There is no Dr. Odlid. There wasn't any Dr. Odlid listed on the directory in the lobby, so I checked out all the faculty offices. There wasn't one for a Dr. Odlid. Then I went to the dean's office. His secretary said there wasn't any Dr. Odlid, so I showed her my grade card. She said it was a joke. I couldn't believe her! 'It's just a prank,' she said. 'This was written on a typewriter. See, I can erase it. The real grade cards are printed. They don't erase.'"

"A joke, huh?" I commiserated.

"Yeah, not very funny. When I find out who the hell did this, they'll wish they had never been born!"

We had planned to confess but this obviously wasn't the right time. In fact, Herbert didn't find out who was responsible until graduation day. I approached him in cap and gown.

"Herb, you remember that thing with Dr. Odlid?"

"Uh-huh."

"I gotta tell you. It was me and the guys across the hall."

He stared at me without a word, turned, and walked off. Some might think our joke was sadistic, but, after all, we were young.

I don't think he ever spelled Odlid backwards.

Bloody Nose

All M1 students took a written final exam on the last day of class. It was an exhaustive number-two-pencil-make-sure-you-fill-in-the-circle-completely multiple-choice test. The questions could be on anything we had covered that year. If you failed, you either dropped out or repeated the first year. It was a stress-inducing situation to say the least. It seems ironic that both my first and last days of the year were disrupted by a bloody nose.

Ever since I was a child, I have had trouble with nosebleeds. Not the typical, small bleed that anybody else gets, but ferocious torrents of blood that seemed to never stop. These kind of bleeds start in what is termed "Kisselbach's Area," a place low on the nasal septum where the arteries lie atypically close to the surface. They can be triggered by minor trauma, excessive nose blowing, dry air, or even by stress. Over the years, I had been treated many times with silver nitrate cautery. Silver nitrate is a caustic chemical, which, when touched to a bleeding area, seals the vessels closed. My problem was that the condition always recurred. Each time, it seemed worse than before.

My first day of medical school was the one and only time I ever wore a white shirt and tie to class. I showered, shaved, and tied a perfect Windsor knot in my best silk tie. As I headed out the door, my nose erupted in a flood of bright red arterial blood, soaking my shirt and tie and then dripping onto the floor and my shoes. I stuffed a tissue in my nostril and applied pressure, but *it would not stop!*

The clock was ticking. The introductory welcome to MCV would start any minute. My nose full of tissue paper, I changed my shirt and tie as fast as possible. I ran to Sanger Hall and took a seat in the rear just as the dean's talk started.

I wouldn't have a severe bleed again until the last day of school.

I felt like I was doing well with the crucial year-end exam. Then, about two-thirds of the way through, my nose started to gush. As so many times before, I stuffed in a tissue, desperately trying to keep blood off the answer sheet, but to no avail. A concerned proctor approached.

"What's wrong with you, Heritage?"

"I'm sorry, I just get these nosebleeds. It will probably stop soon."

"Well, go down to the ENT [Ear, Nose, and Throat] clinic and get it stopped now."

"But I have to finish the test!"

"That's OK. When you come back, we'll give you extra time to finish." Once they had accepted you at MCV, they wanted to keep you.

Off I went to the ENT clinic. Second year students surrounded an Asian resident. "What wrong with you?" he asked.

"I have a nosebleed, and I'm in the middle of taking a test to pass my first year of medical school. Can we please be quick?"

"No problem. We use silver nitrate cautery."

"No, you don't understand. I've had these bleeds all my life and silver nitrate doesn't work. I want electrocautery."

"Hohhh … electlocautely! Hokay! Get in chair."

He stuffed a cocaine pleget in my nose. Cocaine is typically used for ENT work and provides a mild degree of anesthesia. Rummaging in one of the cabinets under the counter, he pulled out a dust-covered electrocautery generator. With its antique black crinkle finish and yellowed voltage gauge, it looked like something left over from Dr. Frankenstein's lab. He plugged it in, spun the dial, and brought the electrode close to the case. A three-inch blue spark zapped out. When he touched it to my nose, my entire body — head to toe — went rigid. It was what the electric chair must (briefly) feel like to the condemned.

"If you do that again," I snarled, "I'm going to kill you!"

Turning to the surrounding students, he remarked "Hohh-hh … medical student make worse patient!"

He turned down the current, and, at my insistence, injected lidocaine, a powerful local anesthetic, into my nasal septum. The rest of the procedure was uneventful. The bleeding finally stopped, and I returned to successfully complete the test.

I had passed my first year of medical school.

The Fan

The second year of school was structured by systems like the first, but it dealt with the diseases of those systems. My friends and I couldn't wait to move out of the dorm.

"I've found us an apartment," Ed announced excitedly. "It's in the Fan!" Ed, Bob, Debbie, Wendy, and I were at dinner in the dormitory dining hall. It was the end of May. Summer recess would start in two weeks. "It's the whole second floor of one of those old buildings on Franklin Street, about a mile from Sanger Hall," he continued. "We can walk to school or, Doug, you can ride your bike."

"Sounds like it's worth taking a look," Bob said. "I hope it's cheap."

"When can we see it?" I added.

"Tomorrow is Saturday," Ed replied. "I'll call the landlady and see if she can meet us there."

"Debbie and I have decided to room together," Wendy said. "Maybe we can find an apartment near you guys."

The Fan is a district in downtown Richmond bordered by U.S. Route 1 in the east and The Boulevard in the west. It's known as "The Fan" because of the way the streets spread out between the two. Monroe Park and the Virginia Commonwealth University undergraduate campus lie on the eastern border. A fashionable address in the late 1800s and early 1900s, many of its stately Edwardian town homes have now been converted into apartments. Cafes, bars, and shops abound on its tree-lined streets. It's an ideal location for students since housing is relatively easy to come by and one can walk to either school. The apartment Ed found was on Franklin Street, one block east of Route 1 and across the street from the exclusive Commonwealth Club, the haunt of successful business men and politicians.

"Are you ready to view the apartment?"

It was Saturday. We stood on the sidewalk looking up at a ramshackle three-story townhouse. The crotchety old landlady, Mrs. Berry, made it clear that she had better things to do.

"Yes, ma'am."

"I don't like renting to students," she announced as we climbed the broken cement steps to the front door. "They have no respect for property. But I suppose I have to, these days. Quality people used to live here. The Fan was quite a nice place when I was a girl. But now it's all hippies. You did say you were medical students, didn't you?"

"Oh, yes ma'am," we sang in unison.

"Well, in that case, I might make an exception."

The gloomy foyer smelled of dust and worm-eaten wood. A creaking staircase, the bannister hanging at a crazy angle, led to the second floor. A narrow dark hall ran the length of the building, a door to the outside at the far end. The staircase continued upward from the landing. "Now, here's the bathroom," she said, leading us down the hall. A toilet, sink, and claw-footed bathtub were the only utilities. Massive cast iron pipes, festooned with cobwebs, ran up one wall. "And here," walking farther down the hall, "is a bedroom." It was perhaps 10 feet by 8 with a cot and antique dresser crammed in.

"This is very nice," I remarked over the smothered snickers of Ed and Bob. "But we were told there was room for three of us."

"In such a hurry!" she snapped. "Back this way." She produced a key at the landing to unlock a side door. We trooped into the kitchen. In the center was a scarred Formica top table and a set of mismatched chairs. To the side was a sink and refrigerator that must have been there since World War II. "Here's the second bedroom," she announced. A door opened from the kitchen to another room. Two mattresses lay on the floor. "And here's the parlor." The front room was a pleasant surprise — spacious with high ceilings, well lit by large bow windows facing onto Franklin Street. It contained a sagging ancient couch and a few beat-up tables and chairs.

"So, do you want to take it or not?"

The place was a hovel, but the location was perfect and, most important, it was cheap. After a brief consultation, we agreed on a one-year lease. "Just remember, boys, when your lease is over, I expect all this furniture to be just as you see it. I won't tolerate any damage!"

"No ma'am," I said. "Of course not. By the way, it seems the only lock is to the kitchen door. Are there keys to the bathroom and other bedroom?"

"No other keys. But this is a very safe neighborhood."

I took the hall room; Ed and Bob shared the room off the kitchen. It must have been a safe neighborhood since anybody could walk in the front door and up the stairs to the bathroom and my bedroom, yet nothing was ever stolen and nobody was molested in the bathtub.

We moved in and immediately set up the all-important stereo and my ancient black and white TV in the parlor. I did most of my studying on the sagging couch. It actually was quite pleasant with the bow windows opened to the summer air. There was constant foot traffic along Franklin Street. Wendy and Debbie rented the second floor of the building next door, which was considerably nicer than ours. School was out and we partied in our new-found freedom almost every night. The parlor shook to rock music, the volume turned to maximum, my Mynah bird shrieking an accompaniment. The bird, JoJo, was supposed to talk, but the only thing he ever said was "Far out," which he must have heard a hundred times a day.

On one occasion, there was a free concert in Monroe Park, only two blocks from us. We sat on blankets, snacked, and drank wine. The music lasted all day and finished that night with a guest appearance by Jerry Lee Lewis. He actually did run his foot down the piano keys. We were having a great time!

A couple of hippies lived next door. The expression "slackers" wasn't in use at that time, but it's a perfect description of those two. They occasionally attended class at VCU but spent most of their time hanging out and selling small amounts of pot. One of them, Jerry, told me an amazing story.

"My brother came back from Vietnam with a bag of Chinese white heroin. That stuff was beyond pure, man!"

"I never figured you for a junkie, Jerry."

"No, man! You're a junkie if you shoot up. No way would I do that!"

"So how do you know it was so pure? Or even heroin, not powdered milk?"

"'Cause, man, we'd like, dip a cigarette into a pile of it and suck some of it up then smoke it like a doobie."

"And that got you high?"

"High ain't the word, man. Like interstellar. Listen to this: one night we got nothing to do, so we just drove around smoking these sticks. My brother's driving, his friend is shotgun. I'm in the back seat when I smell something burning."

"A cigarette fell on the floor and started a fire?"

"No, man! So I look around, there ain't no fire to be seen. Then I look at my hand and the friggin' doobie's burning between my fingers! Shit! It was me on fire! I didn't feel a thing!"

Which goes to show just how powerful a painkiller heroin is. Its medical use is outlawed in the United States. This largely makes sense. It is one of the most addictive substances known. Its illegal use has destroyed uncounted lives. But why not employ it for terminal patients in excruciating pain? Who cares if they're addicted for the last few days or weeks of their lives? That's the policy in Great Britain. Jerry's story made me think.

"The Biograph is running *Deep Throat* tonight," Bob remarked. "Let's get the girls and go!"

The Biograph was an old art theater around the corner on Cary Street. It ran classic movies like *Casablanca* and *Woodstock*. Tickets were cheap. Walking in, one was immediately assaulted by the stale odor of popcorn, perfume, and a tinge of sweat. The five of us were frequent patrons. In 1972, *Deep Throat* was a groundbreaker: the first hard-core porno movie to be shown in public theaters. It aroused an impassioned outcry against obscenity. Under pressure, the Richmond city government banned its exhibition, along with another full-length pornographic film, *The Devil in Miss Jones*. Censorship didn't sit well with the owners of The Biograph, who firmly believed in their First Amendment rights. In protest, they announced a one-night-only screening of *The Devil and Miss Jones* along with *Beaver Valley*. Admittance was free. We didn't attend, but Ed got the scoop the next day.

"People were lined up around the block," he laughed. "A lot of them couldn't get in 'cause all the seats were taken. Then comes on the first movie, *The Devil and Miss Jones*, which turns out to be a 1940s Bob Cummings comedy!"

"Too funny! So what was *Beaver Valley*?"

"A Walt Disney nature film about beavers!"

A lot of people were very irate, but The Biograph was still standing the next day.

Bob Medland

Our neighbors on the floor upstairs gave a New Year's Eve party. The Allman Brothers were blasting overhead. We had a small party of our own in the parlor. The ceiling literally bulged up and down in time to the dancing horde above us.

"That ceiling is going to collapse," I predicted.

"Yeah," said Ed. "Let's hope it doesn't land on any of the furniture!"

In fact, it didn't collapse until the next day, leaving a four-foot hole above and a corresponding mound of plaster and broken lathe below. Thankfully, the pile missed the couch by a foot. We couldn't see any point in cleaning the mess up. It wasn't in the way. We just walked around it.

Later that spring, I was lying on the couch, going over some notes for school, when a strange man appeared in the doorway. He looked to be in his 50s, smartly dressed in suit and tie, standing ram-rod straight.

"What do you want," I snarled.

"I'm General Medland," he snapped.

It was Bob's father! I jumped to my feet as his gaze swept the room, zeroing in on the mound of detritus, scattered dirty clothes, empty beer cans, and overflowing ashtrays.

"Where's Bob," he asked in a menacingly controlled voice.

I had no idea, but it had to sound good. "I believe he's studying at the library, sir."

"When he gets back, tell him I want to talk to him."

General Medland was a three-star air force officer who had just returned from an over-seas command. He arrived at our apartment in a staff car. A sergeant drove him and Bob to dinner that night.

"So, how did it go," I asked as Bob slumped onto the couch.

"Just imagine," was his only reply.

Bob was a great guy but really couldn't hold his liquor. We had a mutual friend, a medical school classmate, also named Bob. Bob Fraker lived east of the Fan, across the street from the Jefferson Hotel, where his roommate was a manager. He and Bob Fraker gave a Christmas Party that year. Debbie, Wendy, Ed, Bob, and I were invited. It was a full-blown formal affair with a bartender, fancy hors d'oeuvres, and a violinist. She was playing a Spanish dance by Sarasate as we arrived. Looking around, we immediately realized we were out of our depth. The room was crowded with older men in tuxedoes and elegant women in fashionable gowns. Trying to make conversation, I approached a mustached gentleman as he harangued his followers in a plummy British accent.

When he paused for breath, I somewhat naively ventured, "You must be English."

"I'm from Detroit," he replied, looking down his nose at me.

How do you respond to that? I quickly made my way over to the bar.

The four of us lowly students stood alone, nibbling appetizers. Wendy and Debbie sipped cocktails. I enjoyed a bourbon on the rocks. Bob was pouring down gin and tonics like they were mother's milk.

"Having a good time?" Bob Fraker sauntered over, a highball in his hand.

"Super, Bob. Merry Christmas! Any other students invited?"

"Just you guys. My roommate was in charge of the guest list. He's made a lot of society friends at work."

"Well, we sure appreciate the invitation," Wendy offered. "It's a great party, but we're going to be late for dinner if we don't leave soon." This was the first I had heard about dinner. I gave Debbie a questioning glance. "That's right," she added, smoothly taking up the ball. "We have reservations at that new Spanish-

Mexican restaurant on Grace Street." Obviously, the girls found the party as boring as I did.

"What's that about dinner?" Bob Medland was working on his third gin and tonic.

"You remember, Bob," Debbie hissed. "The Spanish-Mexican restaurant! Remember?"

Bob finally caught on. "Oh, yeah, I remember now. Let's have another drink before we go!"

"I'm afraid we don't have time. Come on, Bob. Before we're late for our reservation."

"We have a reservation?"

We said goodbye to our host and ushered Bob out as quietly as possible. Fortunately, there really was a Spanish-Mexican restaurant three blocks away. It was about 10 o'clock when we stumbled our way in.

"Do you have a reservation?" asked the maître d'.

"Sure we got a reservation!" blurted out Bob.

"No, we don't," Wendy replied. "Do you have a table for five?"

"But you said we have a reservation!" Bob shouted.

"Shut up, Bob!"

"There's no need for a reservation," the maître d' intervened urbanely. "Please step this way." He led us to a table in the corner, conspicuously away from the other diners. "Your server will be with you shortly."

"We want sangria," Bob demanded. "Do you have any sangria?"

"Certainly, sir. Would you care for a glass or a pitcher?"

"Bring us a pitcher. Wait! Make it two pitchers!"

"One pitcher will be enough for now," Ed told the maître d' with a knowing look. We glanced over the menus.

"I want the enchiladas," Bob announced.

"They're pretty rich. They might not sit well after drinking so much," Debbie warned.

Bob took another gulp of sangria. "But I want enchiladas!"

"Fine, Bob. Have the enchiladas."

The waiter set down our plates. Bob stared at his food for a moment, then fell face down into his plate.

"Bob, Bob, are you OK?" Wendy shouted. Women sometimes ask silly questions in situations such as this.

Our waiter was still standing by. "Can I get you anything else?" he asked solicitously. "Perhaps a stretcher?"

The service at that restaurant really was top drawer.

Horror in the Vending Room

✽

"Let's go fishing!" Bob declared with enthusiasm. An avid hunter and fisherman, he had just bought a new pickup truck, fitted it with a roof rack, and strapped on a brand-new canoe. "How about it, Ed? Wanna go?"

"Some other time," Ed replied, looking up from his class notes. "I've got too much to do today."

"Well, how about you, Doug?"

"I don't know, Bob. I've never been big on fishing. Seems mostly boring to me — sit in a boat for hours, waiting for a bite. Besides, I don't have any tackle."

"Ah, come on. I've got an extra rod you can use and we can share out of my tackle box. And we'll take some beer."

"Where'll we go?"

"Down to the Chickahominy. There's a camp down there with a pier where we can put the canoe in."

The Chickahominy River begins northwest of Richmond and flows to the south, near Williamsburg, before it turns into a swamp. Of significance during the Civil War, it flooded during McClellan's Peninsular Campaign, delaying his army, and giving Robert E. Lee more time to fortify Richmond. I had never been there.

"OK, I'll go. But you buy the beer." Bob's new truck was parked on Franklin Street in front of our apartment, sporting an aluminum canoe on top. We took Route 60 out of Richmond. Traffic was light; most folks going in that direction take Interstate 64. Before long, we were pulling up to a ramshackle bait shop and pier where the river met the swamp. After purchasing some night crawlers, we manhandled the canoe off the roof and slid it into the water.

"Bob, I'm not real comfortable with small boats," I said. "I once had a bad accident in one."

"Just keep your weight in the center. These canoes are a lot more stable than you think."

"So you say," I said, sliding into the rear seat. Bob took the front. Actually, he was right. It seemed stable enough. Getting settled, we each took a paddle and began to move out into the placid river.

"This looks like a good spot for bass," Bob said as we approached a cluster of lily pads. "Let's start casting."

And cast we did. Again and again. Without even a nibble.

"I can see why you love this sport," I said, popping open a beer. "It's so exciting!"

"You just gotta be patient. And quiet. Not like that boat over there."

A Jon Boat carrying a man, woman, and two small children had pulled up about 20 yards away. The kids were making a racket; the wife was loudly hectoring her husband.

"See, the noise goes through the water and scares away the fish. That poor guy won't catch anything," Bob explained with authority. The words were barely out of his mouth when we watched "the poor guy" haul in what looked to be a 10-pound bass. "Maybe we need to move to another spot," Bob muttered.

We moved, but the only thing we caught was a blue gill about four inches long.

"Throw him back," I said with disgust.

"No, we'll use him for bait, like a big minnow," Bob responded. "That should catch a really big one." But it didn't. We still had the tiny fish at the end of the day, our only success. By now, it had expired, and it seemed pointless to throw it back. So we took it home with us.

Back at the apartment, we had to endure a good bit of mockery from Ed and the girls regarding our fishing skills.

"Gee, you guys," Wendy taunted. "We were expecting a big fish fry!"

"Looks like a small meal," Debbie added.

"Yeah, yeah. Small meal. Hey, that gives me an idea!" I said.

"What are you going to do, multiply the fishes, like Jesus?"

"I wish. No, you know the vending room at school, the one off the main lobby? One of those machines sells sandwiches. Cheese, ham and … a fish sandwich! How about if we get a real fish sandwich, take off the wrapper and label and make this guy into a new sandwich? Then we pretend to get it from the vending machine!"

The next day, having procured the requisite real fish sandwich, we did exactly that, laying the tiny fish — head, fins and tail — on a bare hamburger bun, carefully re-wrapping the cellophane and pasting on the label. From the outside it looked just like the real thing. At lunchtime, the vending room was packed as usual, the portly vending room lady busily making change. Planted in the crowd, I watched Ed pretending to use the vending machine as he secretly pulled our "fish sandwich" from under his coat. He unwrapped it to expose what lay within, holding it at arm's length for all to see.

"My God," I pointed and shouted, "Look at that guy's fish sandwich!"

"Uhh, gross!"

"That's disgusting!"

"I think I'm going to be sick!"

All around us, people ripped the cellophane off their sandwiches to check out the contents. One student didn't bother to investigate — she just threw her unopened lunch into the trashcan.

The vending machine lady waddled over to check out the commotion.

"Look at my fish sandwich!" Ed lamented.

"Oh, dear Lord! I'll give you your money back!" We didn't want to take things too far. "No need, ma'am," I explained. "It's just a joke."

"That ain't no joke, honey!" she insisted indignantly.

When I told her what we had done, she let out a great belly laugh and said, "Now why would you nice boys go and do sumpin' like dat?"

Grace Street

*I*n 1973, *The Sting*, starring Paul Newman and Robert Redford, was the top-grossing film. Hard rock had softened considerably; artists like Carly Simon and Elton John led the hit parade. The Supreme Court overturned bans on abortion. It was my third year of medical school.

The third year was our first opportunity to get hands-on experience with patients. Instead of spending four to six weeks in classroom lectures, we were assigned, for similar periods of time, to the various services — Medical, Surgical, Psychiatry, and Obstetrics and Gynecology.

Debbie and I got married at the start of the school year. Wendy was her maid of honor. Bob and Ed were my best men. We moved to a first-floor apartment in an old townhouse on Grace Street. We were still in the Fan and close to our favorite shops and taverns. Our friends stayed on at Franklin Street, close enough for easy and frequent visiting. The couple renting the second floor seemed pleasant enough. Both of them were in their 20s. We exchanged casual greetings as we came and went, but we never became friends and knew nothing about them.

We decorated in the spirit of the old house with kerosene lamps and "antiques" from thrift stores. Our one modern exception was a king-sized waterbed. I opened up the fireplace, and we burned coal on most winter nights. A portrait of my grandfather as a young man hung over the mantle. Debbie completed her Master's degree and got a job in the MCV genetics lab. Now she had time to play the refurbished second-hand upright piano we picked up. I cashed in a life insurance policy to buy our first color TV. I still rode my bicycle to school, now dressed in the whites worn on patient floors. We began to acquire cats. I had a pet cat as a child, and Debbie loved them as well. Kingfish, a solid black kitten, was our first. He was soon followed by Charlie, a seal-point Siamese, then by Tut-tut, a purebred Abyssinian. We took Tut to several cat shows where he won quite a few blue ribbons — when he wasn't acting up. On more than one occasion, he escaped his cage and ran wildly around the arena. Ultimately, we had as many as nine cats sleeping on our bed.

We gave a big Halloween party. We did the best we could on our limited budget, setting out a table with (cheap) liquor and mixers. The refrigerator was stocked with Pabst Blue Ribbon. We laid out bowls of pretzels and potato chips. Debbie baked cookies. She was Cleopatra, and I was Caesar. Bob Medland arrived in a Godzilla suit. Everybody gave a big laugh when Ed and Wendy came in. Ed was bare-chested and wore a diaper. Wendy wore a white lab coat and had on a false beard with a stethoscope around her neck, and play money bulged from her pockets. She was me — the rich obstetrician to be — and Ed was the baby I delivered. Our landlady, Mrs. Glass, made a brief appearance. The cats frantically tore around the house, trying to avoid drunken attempts to pick them up. At the end of the night, the apartment was a mess — empty beer cans, half-finished drinks, and overflowing ashtrays everywhere. But Debbie and I were happy; our first party had been a great success!

Mrs. Glass owned the house next door as well as ours. She lived on the ground floor and rented the upstairs apartment to a group of Greyhound bus drivers who slept there when they had a stopover. Mrs. Glass was a rotund and very nice, if somewhat earthy, lady in her 60s. It was with great relish that she enlightened us regarding our neighbors on the floor above. "They're exhibitionists," she laughed. "Every night they turn on all the lights and draw back the drapes. Then they have sex where everybody can see them. My bus drivers pull up easy chairs to watch and eat popcorn!"

We lived in the Grace Street apartment for five years. When I was a Senior Resident, I was offered a position with an OB-GYN group in Petersburg, Virginia. Debbie and I bought a house in a nice neighborhood, and I commuted to Richmond for the duration of my residency. Our new house had everything we wanted — formal living and dining rooms, a den with a brick fireplace, a spacious kitchen and family room, guest bedrooms, and a master suite. But somehow, I missed our small Grace Street apartment. It was there, in our first home, that Debbie and I were happier than we would ever be again.

Two Faces of Death

"Heritage, wake up!" The intern, Sergio, said as he prodded me in the side. "Time to go to work."

I blearily rose from the chair where I had been napping. "What time is it?"

"It's 2:30."

"2:30 in the morning?" I was only half awake.

"No, 2:30 in the afternoon," was his sarcastic reply. "There must be an eclipse 'cause it's dark outside."

"So, what's up? Some kind of emergency?"

"The emergency is all over. Now we have to go pronounce the patient."

By "pronounce," he meant that as a physician he had to officially declare the patient to be dead. The only dead person I had ever seen, aside from the ones in Gross Anatomy, had been resting peacefully in a casket.

"You need me for this?" I complained.

"Hey, Professor, if I have work to do, so do you. That's why you're on the Medicine rotation. Try to learn something."

It was my third year in school and the first year of actual contact with patients. Internal Medicine was one of the several services we were cycled through, the others being Surgery, Pediatrics, Obstetrics and Gynecology, and Psychiatry. On the Medicine rotation, we were each assigned a number of hospitalized patients to follow. This meant doing physical exams, checking lab and X-ray results, and making notes in the chart, which became part of the permanent record. We made rounds with an intern starting at 6 a.m., followed by rounds with a resident an hour later, and then rounded again on the same patients with an attending doctor at 8. We were expected to answer questions about the conditions of the patients and be familiar with their latest test results. During the day, we were assigned new patients to admit. Our history and physical exams were expected to be quite detailed and had to be signed off by a resident or attending. In the afternoon, rounds were repeated just as in the morning. Students derisively called internists "fleas," because it seemed all they did was jump from one patient to another. Shifts were long and sometimes required an overnight stay.

The West Hospital rotunda, ordinarily a scene of perpetual activity, was eerily quiet. During the day, four elevators constantly ground between the hospital's 12 floors. Now they stood unused and quiet. No gurneys were being wheeled down the halls, no assemblage of white-coated students were to be seen trailing professors, no scuffs on the freshly-waxed floor. The bright lights of the day shifts were dimmed and seemed to have somehow taken on a greenish cast. The air hung thick and heavy around us, as though all the day's motion had been sucked into it. A solitary clerk sat at the nurses' station reading a paperback book.

"You called for someone to do a pronouncement," Sergio stated as we approached her desk.

"Room 923," she replied without looking up.

"Got it."

Corridors branched off in four directions. Sergio chose one, and I followed. Illumination, what there was of it, was fainter, the room numbers hard to read.

"920, 921, 922," he counted. "Ah, here we are. 923." He pushed open the door and barged in.

A stick-thin scarecrow of an old woman lay rigidly on the bed. Her hair was a tangled mess, the color of steel wool that had been used to scrape up a stain. Coffee-colored liquid filled her gaping mouth, leaking slowly from her twisted lips. Her eyes stared in horror at her last view of this world.

"Death by aspiration," Sergio pronounced. "You go get some rest. I'll start the paperwork."

Later that same year, I was assigned to the main emergency room. Widely known as the Saturday Night Gun and Knife Club, it was MCV's main trauma center. Located on the ground floor of the West Hospital, it comprised multiple rooms equipped to deal with simple cuts and lacerations as well as to stabilize victims of more serious injury before transport to surgery. This was where we students got our first experience with cleaning and suturing minor wounds.

"Where is everybody?"

I was reporting for my shift. The ER, ordinarily a hive of activity, looked deserted.

"They're all in the back," the solitary clerk replied.

"What's going on?"

She didn't reply, just shook her head. I made my way to the back. Several attending surgeons as well as all the on-duty residents and interns were clustered around a gurney. On it lay a young girl, nude. She looked to be about 13 or 14. Her hair was long, the color of honey. Her eyes were closed behind two enormous black rings. There wasn't any other mark on her body.

"What happened?" I asked a bystander.

"I think she got hit by a car," she replied. "I didn't get the whole story."

"She's dead?"

"Yeah. See those black eyes? Intracranial hemorrhage. No other injuries. I guess the car almost missed her."

"So what are they doing now?"

"Getting ready to take her upstairs for organ harvest. Her parents signed for kidneys, heart, and corneas."

I had seen two faces of death.

I never wanted to see such things again.

Prolapsed Cord

"Gas just doubled in price," Shelby complained. "Now it's 80 cents a gallon!"

"It's the Arab oil embargo," Carl replied. "You better hope it stays at 80 cents."

The OBG Emergency Room was on the first floor of the old East Hospital. It was here that staff patients — those managed exclusively by the Resident staff — presented when they believed themselves to be in labor. After they registered, patients waited on hard plastic chairs, facing the elevator. There were no newspapers or magazines to keep them entertained. There was no TV. The lobby floor was yellowed linoleum, surely the same laid down when the hospital was built in 1920. Registration forms stating the patient's complaints were passed to the resident in charge, who called for them in order of priority.

Carl was the Senior Assistant Residents (SAR) present. Shelby was an Assistant Resident (AR), one year behind him. It was noon on an ordinary weekday. As usual, other residents, including the Junior Assistants (JARs), were gathered in the East Hospital ER to gossip and shoot the bull. I was one of the students, the "studs," on OB rotation. Studs did the menial "scut work" of drawing blood and starting IVs. When a laboring patient was admitted, she was evaluated by a JAR together with a student. We learned to assess uterine contractions and evaluate the cervix by digital vaginal exam.

As labor progresses, the cervix thins out and dilates. These changes indicate how near the patient is to delivery. If in false labor, the patient would be sent home. If the labor was active, she went to the second floor labor and delivery suite for vaginal birth. There was no Caesarean section facility in the East Hospital. The C-section rooms were on the West Hospital eleventh floor. If a patient failed to progress in labor or otherwise required operative delivery, she was placed on a gurney, taken to the elevator, sent down to the basement, rolled through the steam tunnels to the West Hospital basement, moved back into an elevator, and on up to the eleventh floor.

On this particular day, the unoccupied residents and students were sitting around the front desk idly waiting for something to happen. A registration form came in and was passed to Carl.

"Patient states labor" he read from the form. "Ms. Johnson," he said, addressing a nurse, "would you please take her back and get her ready?"

D.B. Johnson was the charge nurse, a formidable African-American lady of many years seniority. She ruled the ER with an iron hand. Minutes later, she returned.

"She's ready."

"Gunther, you're up," Carl ordered. Conversation continued uninterrupted as the JAR sauntered to the exam room. That is, until we heard, "Oh my God! Prolapsed cord!"

A prolapsed cord is the most extreme of obstetric emergencies. If the bag of water, the amnion, breaks without the fetal head pressed tightly against the lower uterus, the umbilical cord can drop between the head and cervix. With every uterine contraction the cord is squeezed, cutting off blood flow and oxygen to the fetus. If not immediately resolved, the baby will die. There can be no vaginal delivery. A stat Caesarean section is mandatory. But it takes time to get an operating room staffed and ready. Anesthesia must be called, instruments laid out. And this was the East Hospital — no C-section facilities! So it was imperative that pressure be taken off the cord.

The JAR, Gunther, had already followed the standard procedure. He placed the patient in the knee-chest position — on her knees with shoulders on the gurney — which allowed the fetus to slide slightly forward, taking some of the pressure off the cord. Then, climbing onto the gurney behind her, he inserted his hand in her vagina to hold the head up.

I watched in awe as the ER flew into action. There was no panic. Carl, as SAR in charge, calmly fired off orders.

"You," he said to an intern. "Call 11 and tell them we're on the way." To a student: "You, draw blood for a stat type and cross. You," he said to me, "get the chart and bring it along."

Everything was operating smoothly, like a well-oiled machine. The gurney rolled through the swinging doors into the waiting room, the patient on her hands and knees, Gunther behind her, holding the head off the cord. Someone slammed the button to call the elevator. It seemed to take an eternity to arrive.

I was mentally admiring the swiftness with which the crisis was being handled when I noticed that, in our haste, we had forgotten one small detail. She was naked from the waist down, her bare butt up in the air and Gunther crouching behind her with his hand disappearing into her nether region.

We had remembered everything except a sheet to cover her.

The crowded waiting room sat frozen in place, gawking at the spectacle. I heard someone say, "If that's how they do deliveries here, I ain't coming back no more!"

Psychiatry

"**G**ood morning, Mrs. Williams. I'm Dr. Heritage." All students on clinical rotations were referred to as "doctor." I continued, "I'll be helping you for the next several weeks." It was my first day at the outpatient clinic.

Then, M3 Psychiatry rotation was something of a relief after the long hours and endless rounds spent on Medicine and Surgery. Our principal duty was to shepherd pediatric patients on walks around downtown Richmond. There was only one hands-on assignment. Each of us was allocated an outpatient to manage for six weeks. Of course, the psych resident was the real manager. Our responsibility was to meet with the patient, counsel him or her, and write any needed prescriptions. A resident countersigned them after we discussed the case.

"Here's your patient's file," the clerk explained as she handed me a chart several inches thick. "Take your time reviewing it, but remember, the appointment is just for one hour."

I had barely looked at the first few pages when the patient was ushered in.

"It's very nice to meet you, Doctor."

Mrs. Williams was in her late 40s or early 50s. Her dyed black hair was done up tightly in a bun, her lipstick the bright red of a candy-cane. She had on too much rouge. Her cheeks were plastered with makeup in a forlorn attempt to conceal wrinkles spreading like a dry riverbed. Glancing at the chart, I saw that she worked for the Richmond City Government.

"How are you today?" I queried, just fishing. I had no idea why she was in therapy.

"I don't think I'm doing very well."

"I'm sorry to hear that. What's bothering you?"

"I'm having trouble at work. Nobody likes me. The people there talk behind my back. I couldn't find an important file the other day. I'm sure one of them hid it to spite me!"

"Why do you think that?"

"Oh, it's true, doctor. I know because Jesus told me."

"Jesus told you?"

"Yes he did. I talk with Jesus every day, and he tells me all about the nasty things they do and say behind my back!"

At this point, I decided it would be a good idea to look a little deeper into her chart. It was quickly apparent that she was a schizophrenic. A previous doctor had prescribed Stellazine — a major antipsychotic, but not as sedating as Thorazine.

"Mrs. Williams, I see that the last time you were here, the doctor wrote you a prescription. Have you been taking a little blue pill?"

"No I haven't. I told that doctor there was nothing wrong with me, and I didn't need any of her medicine."

The interview continued in a similar vein until it was time to finish up. I felt I had established a degree of trust.

"Mrs. Williams," I said, "I'm afraid our time is up, but I must say that I've greatly enjoyed our little talk."

"I'm so glad you feel that way, doctor. You seem to understand my problems, not like some of the other doctors here."

"I'm pleased you feel that way. You know, I think that blue pill might be just the thing to set things right. If I write you a prescription, will you take it every day? As a favor to me?"

"Yes, doctor. If you say so, I'll do that."

"Great! Let's plan to see you back in two weeks."

Clearly, she was suffering from a mild form of paranoid schizophrenia. I wrote her a prescription for Stellazine. Excusing myself, I left to discuss her case with the resident, Jock (who reappears in the story "Folie à Deux"). He agreed that resuming the medication was appropriate and countersigned the prescription.

Two weeks later, she was back.

"Good morning, Mrs. Williams. How are you today?"

"I'm just fine, doctor."

"And how are things going at work?"

"Oh, they're ever so much better! Nobody is talking about me behind my back and — you know that missing file? Will you believe it, it was on my desk all the time under some other papers!"

"That's wonderful! And are you taking that blue pill I prescribed?"

"Oh yes, just like you told me, I take it every day. There's just one problem, though."

"What's that?

"Jesus doesn't talk to me anymore."

Unless you have actually been in the presence of a psychotic, it is hard to comprehend how real their delusions are for them. A neurotic may suffer from unreasonable fears, but still is in contact with reality. The hallucinations of a psychotic are as reasonable to them as the fact that the sun comes up in the morning. Mrs. Williams truly believed Jesus spoke with her. She had no idea that it was all in her mind. Likewise, she had no idea that the little blue pill had anything to do with Jesus' silence.

My exposure to full-blown psychosis was one of the most interesting and illuminating episodes of my medical education.

Mrs. Williams really was a very nice and somewhat amusing lady. I was pleased and gratified that I was able to help her.

Later, on the same rotation: "Heritage, we have a new admission. Just arrived. A boy. I want you to go do an intake interview."

"Sure! Where is he now?"

"In the secure facility, West Hospital."

"Where's that?"

"In the basement."

An orderly met me outside the lock-up. He was a very large black man in whites — think of "Barney" in *Silence of the Lambs*.

I introduced myself: "Hi, my name is Heritage, third year med school on the psych rotation. I'm supposed to interview the kid that just got admitted."

"Is that a fact? OK, he's in there," he replied, pointing to a steel door that the hospital probably acquired second hand when Alcatraz was abandoned. "Just knock on the door when you want to come out." The heavy door groaned as he heaved it open. I stepped inside. The small room was bare except for a cot and a 40 watt bulb in a metal cage. Huddled in the corner was a muscle-bound teenager wearing a hospital johnny.

I introduced myself in a less formal manner: "Hi, my name is Doug. I'd like for us to have a chat."

"Urrghhh," he replied.

"Sorry, I didn't get that. What did you say?"

"Aarrrggggg," he growled, rising from the floor. He must have been a basketball player, being well over 6 feet tall.

"There's no need to get upset! Really! I'm here to help you!"

"Grrr ... ugghhh ... grrrr," he howled, beginning to advance. That was enough for me, interview be damned. I pounded on the door.

"OK, OK, I'm done here! Let me out! Now!"

The warder chuckled as he swung the door open.

I had nothing to compare with this experience until, some years later, I saw the Mel Brooks movie, *Young Frankenstein* (1974), during which Gene Wilder gets locked in with the monster.

First Pelvic Exam

"Ms. Jackson," I called. "Ms. Jackson! Is Ms. Jackson here?"

"She's not here," said the nurse.

It was my first day assigned to the Outpatient Gynecology Clinic as part of my third-year OBG rotation. It dealt with minor problems. Most of the women there wanted birth control; some had vaginal infections. I was one of three students assigned to follow a resident and learn the basics of office-based gynecology. It was to be my first experience with a pelvic exam.

The female pelvis is shaped like a broad, deep bowl containing the uterus, Fallopian tubes, and ovaries. Unless abnormally enlarged by disease, these organs can't be felt by pressing on the abdomen alone. A gynecologist must insert two fingers into the vagina and lift up on the cervix. By doing so, the uterus and ovaries can be palpated by laying the other hand on the belly, just above the pubis. That, at least, is the theory behind the pelvic exam. With a little practice, it's not too difficult to outline the organs in a reasonably thin woman. As the subject's weight goes up, it becomes more problematic.

For teaching purposes, each student took a form from the top of the pile, interviewed the patient, and, with the assistance of a nurse, performed an exam. Then, we presented our findings to a resident who, in turn, performed their own exam, after which we were, usually, corrected. The clinic was a valuable experience, as it mimicked the day-to-day experience of most gynecologists in private practice.

I called for my patient again.

"She's not here," said the nurse.

"Why not? She's registered."

"She's in the laundry room."

"Why is she in the laundry room?"

"Because our scale only goes up to 300 pounds. We had to send her down to the laundry room to be weighed on their scale."

Ms. Jackson eventually lumbered in. She was enormous! Her breasts were the size of Halloween pumpkins! Her paunch hung halfway to her knees!

"Nurse, would you please get Ms. Jackson ready for examination?" I asked with trepidation.

"Of course, doctor," the wicked old nurse, who had seen generations of medical students pass through, replied with bare-ly-concealed unctuous glee. The exam table creaked and shook as the patient hoisted herself onto it.

"Good morning, Ms. Jackson. I'm Dr. Heritage. I see that you're here for birth control pills."

"Yes, Doctor," she tittered. "I have a new boyfriend, and he doesn't want any children." When she laughed, her breasts bounced up and down like a bobble-head doll.

"Certainly," I replied. Seating myself at the foot of the exam table, I helped fit her heels into the stirrups. Each thigh alone must have weighed 100 pounds.

"I'm going to put a speculum in your vagina to see your cervix and take a PAP smear."

Speculums were available in four sizes — very small for children, small and medium for average-sized women, and an 8-inch one for obese patients. I started with the gigantic one, but try as hard as I could, it would not reach the cervix. I abandoned the plan to do a PAP. If it was essential, the resident could darn well do it. Inserting my fingers in her vagina, I made a half-heart-ed attempt to feel the uterus — to no avail. It was like trying to outline a pea in the middle of a big, overstuffed pillow.

"OK, Ms. Jackson. I'm all done here. Another doctor is go-ing to do his own exam and write you a prescription for birth control pills."

"Thank you, Dr. Heritage. You've been very nice. I know I'm a little on the large side, but you never said a word about my weight!"

I smiled and left the room.

"Sorry," I told the supervising resident. "My fingers are barely 6 inches long. I couldn't even reach the cervix."

"Don't worry," he laughed. "The chief of the department couldn't have done any better."

First Delivery

"OK, Doug," Shelby said, "Go ahead and examine her. Tell me what position the fetus is in."

It was to be my first delivery. I had followed the patient since her admission through the East Hospital ER. This was not her first baby. She had two young children at home. She was what we termed a "multigravida," as opposed to someone pregnant for the first time — a "primigravida." As a multigravida, I expected her labor to be quick, followed by an easy delivery. I was glad that Shelby was my mentor. An easy-going fellow from southern Virginia, he always took his time with students and never lost his temper. We were in the second-floor delivery room. The patient was on the table, prepped, draped, with her feet in the stirrups.

Frankly, I can't remember the woman herself. She may have been white, black, or Hispanic — it made no difference to me. I just wanted to get through the delivery without screwing up. I had watched residents perform several deliveries. Now, it was my turn. I put two fingers in her vagina and felt for the fontanelles. The fetal skull isn't solid; it's made of six separate bony plates that can overlap, allowing the head to squeeze through the birth canal. The gaps between the plates are called the fontanelles. One can determine the orientation of the fetal head by palpating them.

"They're in a vertical line," I replied. "So, the head is in the anterior-posterior position." The A-P attitude lets the head slip through the constricted space at the bottom of the pelvis.

"Right. A couple of pushes is all it'll take."

And a couple of pushes was all it took.

I stood at the foot of the table, gowned, gloved, and masked, holding a sterile towel. The head began to crown at the distended vaginal opening. I pressed the towel against her perineum, between the vagina and anus, to reduce the chances of tearing. The head slipped out, looking at the floor.

"Now," Shelby instructed, "some gentle rotation." The shoulders were still in the birth canal, cross-wise, or transverse. They needed to be A-P to pass through the tight space. Grasping the head, I gently turned it to face the left. The shoulders popped out, immediately followed by the body.

"Clear the airway," Shelby said.

I turned the slippery baby head down and smacked its bottom. The newborn began to wail. I used a suction bulb to clear some remaining amniotic fluid from the airway.

"Clamp the cord."

I used two plastic clips to clamp the umbilical cord and cut between them to free the baby. A nurse immediately took her to a warmer. Using a syringe, I drew cord blood. The placenta was still in the uterus. The delivery would not be complete until it was out.

"Should I pull on the cord?" I asked.

"Just enough to keep it taunt," Shelby replied. "Too much and it'll break. Just wait. You'll feel the placenta separate."

A few minutes later, the placenta was in my hands amidst a gush of blood.

"Is it intact?"

It was in one piece.

"Looks like it's all here," I replied.

"OK, check for lacerations."

Using a speculum, I examined the vagina and cervix. No damage.

Shelby shook my hand. "Congratulations, Doug! Well done!"

I took off my gown and gloves and went over to the warmer. I know that newborns can't focus their eyes, but I swear she looked at me as if to say, "Thank you for bringing me into the world." I put a finger in her little hand and felt her tiny, perfect fingers squeeze mine.

I am often asked how many babies I have delivered. I never counted, but after my experience as a student, resident, and 36 years of private practice, it must be in the thousands. Every one, in its own way, was special. But I don't think any of them gave me the same pride and joy as my first.

The Surgical Rotation

"What are you thinking, Heritage?" Dr. Smith asked. It was 2 a.m. and I had been holding a retractor for four hours. I was literally asleep on my feet.

A third-year student, I was on the Surgical Rotation assigned to Red Surgery, which dealt with vascular procedures. Students were randomly allocated among the various surgical sub-specialties, which also included Gastrointestinal, Orthopedic, and Neurosurgery. Gowned and gloved, we scrubbed in on operations to hold retractors and learn sterile technique. Confined to the foot of the operating table, we could rarely see the incision, which was obscured by the chief and assistant surgeons as well as the scrub nurse passing instruments. Consequently, we came out of the OR with gloves as clean as when we put them on. This was dubbed as "being Snow Whited," as in "Ed, I got Snow Whited today after standing for three hours."

Saint Betery was the senior resident in charge of Red Surgery. A Hungarian immigrant, he was still in training after having completed college, medical school, an internship, and five years of general surgery. A tall, good-natured guy, his thinning hair reflected the many years he had devoted to the demanding specialty of vascular surgery. I liked him enormously and enjoyed imitating his thick Hungarian accent for my classmates' amusement. He seemed to like everybody except Russians, which was understandable since he had lived through the Hungarian revolt against Soviet occupation.

Rounds began each morning at 6 a.m. Going from bed to bed, we observed junior residents presenting their patients to Saint Betery. Surgery started at 8 a.m. and typically lasted until late afternoon. Then, it was off to the Radiology file room to check out that day's X-rays. Then came evening rounds. If you were lucky, you got to go home for a few hours of sleep and then repeat it all in the morning.

On one occasion, I wasn't so lucky.

"Dr. Smith has scheduled an emergency surgery," Saint Betery announced. We had just finished evening rounds. It was 8 p.m. "I'm assisting him, and we need a student as well. I know it's late and you all want to go home, but do I have a volunteer?"

In the Army, you never volunteer for anything, but I was never in the Army. I liked surgery. I liked Saint Betery. I raised my hand.

"So, Dr. Heritage. Good. Go get something to eat and meet us in half an hour."

Dr. Smith was waiting outside OR 8. He was of medium height and wore gold-rimmed glasses. His hair was coal black, tinged with gray. I guess he was in his 40s. "Hi," he said with a smile. "Lazlo said he had a student volunteer. You must be Heritage."

"Yes, Sir."

"Did he tell you what we're going to do?"

"No, Sir."

"It's a parathyroidectomy. You know about the parathyroid glands?"

"Only that they control calcium levels in the body."

"Right. Our patient tonight has a benign parathyroid tumor, and it's out of control. If it's not removed immediately, she may die."

Saint Betery joined us. He went into lecture mode as we scrubbed. "As you already know, Doug, there are four parathyroid glands in the neck, two on each side of the trachea. They're normally between the size of a grain of rice or a bean."

"Removing them sounds simple enough," I replied naively.

"The problem is, they're buried in fat and lymph nodes. The glands look just like the lymph nodes. Anything we remove has to go to Pathology for frozen section to be sure."

"But the Pathology Lab is in the basement."

"And we are on the eleventh floor. That's the problem."

The patient was already under. A rolled up towel under her neck supported her head, which was arched back exposing her throat. Dr. Smith made the first incision and handed me a retractor. After about 15 minutes, he produced a tiny glob of yellowish tissue on the end of his forceps. A nurse took it off to send to Pathology. Thirty minutes later, the report came back: lymph node.

This went on again and again for hours.

"What are you thinking, Heritage?" Dr. Smith asked. It was 1 a.m. I had been standing for four hours and was literally asleep on my feet.

Jolted awake, I blurted out without thinking, "Dr. Smith, I'm thinking I could have watched *Gone with the Wind* while you did this operation!"

They both doubled up with laughter.

"OK, Doug," Saint Betery said when he recovered. "I think Dr. Smith and I can finish up here without you. Go on home."

Plastic Surgery

"Here's the call schedule for the next six weeks," Dr. Theogaraj said as he passed the papers out.

It was 1975, my fourth year of medical school. Betamax and VHS video tape recorders had just been introduced. The inflation rate was over nine percent. Nixon had resigned in disgrace, and Gerald Ford was president. It was my first day on a new rotation. The chief of the Plastic Surgery Department, Dr. Theogaraj, and two plastic surgery fellows were present. They were both in their late 30s and already starting to go gray. After four years of medical school, a year of internship, and five years of general surgery, only now were they finally training in their chosen specialty.

My fourth year was completely elective since I had performed satisfactorily during the first three. I had already decided to go into OB-GYN and loaded my schedule with electives in that field. Being naturally lazy, I had also signed up for six weeks on plastic surgery. I figured it wouldn't entail too much effort. Certainly, I wouldn't do any surgery or be responsible for patients! My confidence evaporated as I studied the call schedule.

"Dr. Theogaraj," I said, "there must be some mistake. According to this, I'm alternating every third night with the Fellows. Who's really on call for the nights I'm assigned?"

"Just like it says. You're on call."

"Ohhhh-kay. What do you do when you're on call?"

"You make rounds on the plastic surgery ward and write any orders needed," he replied. "You do pre-op exams on the patients scheduled for surgery in the morning. And you're on call to the ER for any injuries that require a plastic surgeon."

"Dr. Theogaraj, I'm just a fourth year student! I don't have a medical license! How can I cover the ER? I don't know anything about plastic surgery!"

"You'll learn," he said with a smile. "One of the Fellows will countersign your orders. They'll help out in the ER if you need them."

Well, learn I did. It was sink or swim, and I was determined not to sink. The department had a great library. There were many textbooks and films illustrating procedures I might need when by myself in the ER. I scrubbed in on every operation. At the start of the rotation, I simply observed and held retractors. As time went by, I was allowed to do more. With each step in a procedure, the surgeon described what he was doing and then let me try my hand at it. Every third night, I rounded on the ward, wrote orders, did physicals, and then retired to the library to bring myself up to speed. I slept in the residents' quarters as best one can when the phone might ring at any moment. The nurses on the ward, as well as the patients, called me "Doctor Heritage." I took pride in my newfound responsibility.

The phone rang at 3:30 a.m. one night towards the end of my six-week rotation.

"This is the ER," the desk clerk announced. "You're needed."

Rubbing the sleep from my eyes, I made my way to the trauma ER. "What's up?" I mumbled.

"Auto accident. He hit the windshield. No major damage, vitals are OK. You need to sew up his ear; then he can be discharged home."

"No problem."

The patient was in a minor trauma room, heavily sedated, his face a mask of blood. His left earlobe was split down the center. I called for a plastic surgery tray and did the repair, as taught, with fine nylon sutures 1 millimeter from the skin edge and 2 millimeters apart. It took about half an hour.

"Done," I thought. "Now back to bed." Taking another look at his bloody face, I decided I couldn't let him go home looking like something from a horror movie. I cleaned him off with wet towels, exposing a horseshoe-shaped wound on his left cheek.

"OK, they missed this when they brought you in," I thought to myself.

Probing the cut with surgical tweezers, I pulled out a dagger-shaped piece of broken glass a half-inch wide and three inches long.

"Nice going, ER," I thought.

Obviously, this had to be repaired. I should have called for one of the Fellows, but by this time, it was 4:30 — the very worst time to be routed out of bed. I debated handling it myself. The problem was the horseshoe cut. A horseshoe can't simply be sewn up or it will leave a large puckered scar. From my reading, I knew that the entire defect had to be excised along Langer's lines — the natural folds in the skin. That could be closed in a straight line, leaving a fine scar resembling a facial wrinkle.

"Bring me another plastics tray," I called to the nurse.

After cleaning the defect with Betadine and injecting local anesthesia, I used a scalpel to cut a piece out of his face about one inch long and a half-inch wide. I closed the defect with nylon sutures and put on a dressing.

Then it hit me — I had exceeded my authority to an unimaginable degree! There surely would be repercussions. I decided to admit the patient and face up to what I'd done on morning rounds.

I joined Dr. Theogaraj and the Fellows for rounds at 7 a.m. We progressed from bed to bed exchanging comments and questions on each patient.

"Who's this?" Dr. Theogaraj asked when we came to my ER patient.

"It's a patient from the ER last night," I explained. "Auto accident. They called me to repair his ear but missed a piece of glass in his face. It left a horseshoe. It was late, and I didn't want to bother anybody, so I elliptically excised it."

I held my breath. Now was when the storm would come down.

"I see." Dr. Theogaraj gently peeled off the dressing and studied my repair. "Very good. Next patient," he said.

That was the highest compliment ever paid to me in medicine.

A Big Mistake

"Get off the damn bed, Heritage!" Don Hale shouted. It was lunchtime and the West Hospital residents' room was packed, including myself and some friends of mine. We were in our fourth year of school. The "luxurious" residents' room opened off of Labor and Delivery. It was about 8 by 10 feet. It contained a desk, an ancient TV, and two chairs. The only other furniture was a double-decker bunk bed. There had to be at least 10 people crowded in when I arrived.

Don Hale, a senior resident soon to finish the program, sat at the desk. The other chair was occupied, as was the lower bunk. An open attaché case lay on the top bunk, but there was plenty of free space beside it. I boosted myself up, jostling the case but not spilling anything. Hale was notorious for his condescending and noxious attitude towards anybody his junior.

"Get off the damn bed, Heritage!" he shouted. "And you better not disturb my brief case!"

I had had minor run-ins with Hale before, but now I let the notorious Heritage family temper, like an evil twin, take possession of me. It was a big mistake.

"Don, I didn't disturb your freaking briefcase, and I have just as much right to be here as you!" The room went dead silent. Hale just stared at me for a moment, then got up without a word and walked out.

One of the Assistant Residents came over to stand beside the bed. "You know where he's going, don't you?" he said quietly.

"I don't care where he's going."

"Well, you should. I know him, and I guarantee he's on his way to Dr. Dunning (the Chief of Service) to complain about you. I think you just kissed your chances at a JAR slot goodbye."

I debated whether to go see Dr. Dunning and try to explain the situation or say nothing. I decided to say nothing. I didn't want to be a crawling petitioner when I felt I was in the right. But as days passed, I began to get the cold shoulder from residents I considered my friends and downright hostility from the others. I made an appointment to see Dr. Dunning.

"Dr. Dunning," I began. "A situation has come up that I need to tell you about."

"What situation is that, Douglas?"

"Well, it seems that I've made an enemy of Don Hale."

"How so?" I explained what had happened in the residents' room. "And I'm getting the feeling that I might be passed over for the JAR position."

He stared at me with pale blue eyes that might have been chipped off an iceberg.

"Douglas, as you know, one generally serves an internship before being considered for the Residents Program."

"Yes, sir, I know that. But I understand that, occasionally, one can go straight to Junior Resident. That's why almost all of my electives this year have been in obstetrics or gynecology. I think — I hope — that I already have the experience that an intern would have."

"No decisions have been made yet. You will be notified of your status in due course."

"Thank you, sir."

I left his office with a very bad feeling.

House staff appointments start on July 1. During the first week of June, I was offered an internship position. I could have declined and gone elsewhere, but Debbie and I were comfortably settled in Richmond. I accepted. Another of my classmates, Rebecca, took over as JAR. My friends commiserated with me but knew that I had brought this on myself by antagonizing Don Hale.

I spent all of July and half of August as an intern on the Medical service and in the Emergency Room. I heard on the grapevine that Rebecca was having difficulties with her new position. Then I got a summons to Dr. Dunning's office.

"What now?!" I thought.

Dr. Dunning seemed embarrassed. "Doug, I'm afraid that Rebecca has had a nervous breakdown. It seems she couldn't handle the responsibility. She's dropped out. I need four Junior Residents to run the program. Would you like the position?"

Of course I accepted.

After finishing at MCV, Don Hale had taken a Fellowship in Gynecologic Oncology at a prestigious Florida hospital. He returned to Richmond to join the faculty when I was a Senior Resident. Everybody knew our history and gleefully expected fireworks between us, but I was determined not to indulge their *schadenfreude*. Fortunately, we were on different services and had no need to work together. Occasionally, we would pass in the corridor, our conversation limited to:

"Dr. Hale."

"Dr. Heritage."

I had finally learned to keep my mouth shut.

~ PART 3 ~

Internship and Residency

Folie à Deux

*I*t was 1976. Apple was a new start-up company. The Bee
Gees were disco kings. The supersonic Concorde made its
first flight. The Viking 1 space probe landed on Mars. I was an intern assigned to the West Hospital ER. Shifts alternated between
12 and 16 hours. I worked in a fog of fatigue and don't remember
many details. Only two patients stand out.

The first was the tick lady.

Her complaint was having been bitten by a tick. She had arrived by ambulance.

"It says here that you were bitten by a tick," I said, reviewing her registration form.

"That's right! I need to be checked for Rocky Mountain spotted fever." The disease had recently been in the news. All the cases were in the far West.

"Where's the tick?"

"I pulled it off."

"When did this happen?"

"'Bout a half hour ago."

"So you thought you needed an ambulance?"

"Yeah, and I want to be checked for Rocky Mountain spotted fever right now!"

"Well, in the first place, there haven't been any reports of Rocky Mountain spotted fever in Virginia, so it's very unlikely that the tick was infected. Second, even if it had been, any test for it now would be negative. It takes several days for the infection to take hold and the test to turn positive."

"I don't care! I want to be tested *right now*!" she yelled.

"I'm sorry, I'm not going to order that."

"What's your name? I'm gonna call my lawyer!"

"It's Heritage, just like it says on my name badge. Be sure to spell it right."

The second memorable patient wasn't irritating, just fascinating. Her name was Gloria Schmidt, and her registration stated "pain in knee." She was an unremarkable-appearing lady in her early 40s, nicely dressed and made-up. In the examining room, she lifted her skirt to reveal a swollen, red knee.

"So, what happened to your knee, Ms. Schmidt? Did you fall on it?" I asked.

"No, I didn't fall."

No further explanation.

"Did you twist your leg somehow?"

"No, I didn't twist my leg."

When patients are evasive about an injury, the most likely explanation is abuse.

"Did someone hurt you? Maybe someone you know?"

"Certainly not!" she exclaimed indignantly.

"Look," I said. "Obviously something happened to your knee. How can I help you if you won't help me?"

"If I tell you, you won't tell anybody else?"

"Everything you tell me is confidential."

"All right. The fact is that the CIA has been broadcasting gamma rays into my knee!"

I was so taken aback that for a moment, I didn't know what to say.

"The CIA. Gamma rays."

"That's right! And believe me, it's not just the CIA. The FBI are part of it too! They've been persecuting me for years!" She stroked her knee tearfully. "Now look what they've done to me!"

"I see. Yes, that looks very painful. By the way, is anybody here at the hospital with you?"

"Yes, my mother is in the waiting room."

"Please excuse me for a minute." I went out to the waiting room and found a little old lady, her blue-gray hair coiled in a tight bun, an enormous satchel at her side. "Hello Ms. Schmidt. I'm Dr. Heritage. I've been taking care of your daughter."

"Hello, Doctor," she replied with a slight German accent. "How is she doing?"

"That's what I wanted to talk to you about. How long has she had these delusions that the government is after her?"

"Delusions! What do you mean, delusions?" she snapped in outrage.

"Well, she thinks the CIA is broadcasting gamma rays into her knee!"

"And you don't believe her? Let me tell you — it's not just her! They're after me, too!"

Rummaging through her satchel, she pulled out a thick sheaf of papers and handed them to me. "See for yourself," she said smugly. They were letterheads, all stamped with the official seals of the FBI and CIA. Each one began in a similar manner — something to the effect of "In regard to your request under the Freedom of Information Act, we wish to inform you that this agency has no files in respect to you or your daughter."

"See," she said. "They all lie. They claim there are no files, but that's a lie. And that's not all. I think we were followed to this hospital. They have to keep the gamma rays top secret. They can't let the public know what they're up to. They're afraid my daughter might tell somebody about them."

There is a psychiatric diagnosis known as *folie à deux*. It's one of those conditions taught in medical school but, like Wilson's disease or Schistosomiasis, you never expect to encounter it in real life. It occurs when two psychotics are living together. Sometimes, they start to share the same delusion, feeding on and reinforcing each other. Thus, the French name loosely translated into "craziness of two."

I excused myself from the mother, went back to the ER, and called my friend Jock, the psychiatry resident. "Hi, Jock. It's Doug Heritage in the ER. You won't believe what I've got down here. There's a mother and daughter, and they're both crazy as bedbugs. You need to come down here and lock them up."

"Are they violent? Have they hurt anybody or threatened to?"

"No, no, it's a case of *folie à deux*. You gotta see it!"

"Doug. If they're not a threat to themselves or others, we can't just lock them up. But it does sound interesting. I'm on my way."

"Great! Tell you what — I'm going to tell the patient that you're a knee specialist I've called in."

Jock was there in a few minutes. He finished interviewing the younger Ms. Schmidt, and then he spoke with her mother. It didn't take him long to agree with my diagnosis.

"Doug, you're right. It's a classic case, but they're harmless. I gave the daughter a shot of Prolixin [used to treat schizophrenia] and told her it was for the knee. I also gave her a prescription for painkillers and an appointment for both of them to see me in the clinic next week. But, you know, they probably won't keep it."

As far as I know, they never did.

First Operation

❧

"The West Hospital needs someone for a postpartum tubal," Bryan said. We were sitting in the East Hospital ER. Nothing much was going on. "Do you want to do it, Heritage?" It was early in my first year as a resident. I had assisted on several of these procedures and been the first surgeon on a few, always with an AR assisting me. I had never done one by myself without back-up on the other side of the table.

"Sure, I'll do it."

"Do you want me to go with you?"

"Nah, I'm fine with it," I replied complacently.

"OK. If you run into any problems, call me."

"Sure thing."

At MCV, residents performed routine surgery on staff patients, usually without the assistance or oversight of a faculty member. The first operation that a Junior Assistant Resident learned was postpartum tubal ligation. The joke at MCV was "see one, do one, teach one." That was an exaggeration, of course, but at the Medical College of Virginia — a big city hospital with a large indigent population — we rapidly got a lot of experience. Postpartum sterilization is a simple operation well within the capabilities of junior residents. After assisting on the procedure as a student and in the first months as a new JAR, it was time to go solo.

Nowadays, almost all tubal sterilizations are done with a laparoscope. A telescope is inserted and through a tiny incision and the Fallopian tubes cauterized, ringed, or clamped. In fact, gynecologists invented laparoscopy. In the 1970s, its only use was sterilization. Since then, laparoscopy has been co-opted by other surgical services and largely supplanted most of the old open procedures. But in 1977, when I was a JAR, most sterilizations were done within a few days following delivery. The operation was called a Pomeroy Tubal Ligation after the doctor who first described it.

After delivery, the uterus shrinks, or involutes. By the second or third day, the top, or fundus, lies at the level of the navel and can be easily felt with a hand on the abdomen. With the patient under general anesthesia, the surgeon makes a transverse incision — about an inch long — along the lower edge of the umbilicus. The opening is extended into the pelvic cavity. Using a finger, a Fallopian tube is hooked up and pulled into view. A loop is made, cut, and tied. The same thing is done on the opposite side. The incision is closed and a dressing is applied. The whole thing takes about 20 minutes.

I made my way to the West Hospital full of self-assurance. I could do this surgery in my sleep! The first blow to my confidence came as I walked into the operating room.

"Where's the Assistant Resident?" demanded Ms. Jinter. She was head scrub nurse for the whole nursing staff, famous for her obsequious kowtowing to the professors and a terror to the residents.

"The AR's not coming. I'm doing this one myself," I replied.

"Mmmm-hmmmm," she said, giving me the fish eye.

Legend had it that while one of the senior professors was operating, he needed a particular instrument from the Mayo stand. Mrs. Jinter's back was turned away, so the assisting resident reached over to grab it. Mrs. Jinter whirled around and smacked the resident's hand with an 18-inch stainless steel retractor.

"Don't you ever touch my Mayo stand," she snarled.

"You double-damned hag," the resident shouted. "If you ever do that again, I'll kill you!"

"Doctor, did you hear what he said?" she whined. "Did you hear what he called me?"

"I certainly did!" The professor turned to the resident. "Don't you ever speak to a nurse like that again! Remember your place!" Then he turned to Mrs. Jinter: "You double-damned hag! If you ever do that again, I'll kill you!"

I glanced at the instrument setup. All plain stainless steel. A world-famous gynecologist, an eminent teacher, and an author of textbooks had once been invited to MCV to demonstrate a unique operation. Mrs. Jinter made sure all his instrument handles were gold-plated. I didn't get any of those.

Taking my time at the scrub sink, I mentally walked through every step of the procedure. It's simple, I told myself. No problem. By now, anesthesia had the patient under. I stepped to the table and carefully draped her, leaving only a few inches around the navel uncovered.

Then, I stood frozen in place! My mind was blank! I knew what I was supposed to do — make an incision, find the tubes, and tie them — but exactly how one went about doing this had departed.

Mrs. Jinter fidgeted impatiently, waiting for me to request an instrument. Standing like a statue, I desperately tried to remember the procedure. "It's simple," I thought. "You just…" Nothing.

I could feel the Anesthetist staring at me, wondering what the delay was. A clock in my head was ticking, ticking. The hair on the back of my neck stood up. It was like someone had poured a bucket of ice water over me. Mrs. Jinter snorted "Mmmm-hmmmm" knowingly. Should I stop and call Bryan for help? I would be the laughing stock of the East Hospital. I had to muddle through somehow.

I asked for a scalpel. I knew I had to start with that. As I made the first incision, some details began to come back. Frankly, I don't remember the rest of the operation, but I got it done. As far as I know, the patient never got pregnant. But I do know that my technique was somewhat unorthodox — if filmed, it would be called the Heritage Tubal Ligation.

"How'd it go?" Bryan asked, back at the East Hospital.

"No problem," I said.

Labor and Delivery

"You have got to be kidding! Did you use leeches and blood-letting as well?"

I was talking to a newly minted OBG about my training at MCV. She had just finished her residency and accepted a place with a large local group. Reminiscing about my training in the '70s made me think about how dramatically the practice of obstetrics had changed, largely due to three developments: ultrasound, fetal monitoring, and the use of epidural anesthesia.

It is essential to accurately know the gestational age of the fetus, meaning how long it has been in the womb since conception. A baby born between 37 and 41 weeks is considered full term and is expected to be healthy. Prior to 37 weeks, it is premature. Past 41 weeks, it is at risk of stillbirth.

Babies delivered early that are viable — anywhere from 24 to 36 weeks — are prone to complications, ranging from blindness and brain injury (for the most premature) to minor and easily dealt-with problems as they get closer to maturity.

After 41 weeks, the placenta begins to fail. When it can no longer provide enough oxygen, the result is fetal death.

For hundreds of years, doctors and midwives relied on a patient's history to determine gestational age. Using information such as the date of the last menstrual period, the onset of morning sickness, when fetal motion was first felt, and the size of the uterus, they could arrive at an approximate due date. Unfortunately, their crude estimates were often wrong.

The introduction of ultrasound in obstetrical practice was revolutionary. A picture of the fetus could be produced using high-pitched sound waves, something like a ship using sonar to map the ocean floor. Measurements taken from the picture, such as the width of the head and the crown to rump length, enabled obstetricians to date a fetus with precision. The first crude ultrasound machine arrived at MCV when I was a senior resident. Unlike modern machines, which use an array to create a real-time picture, it used a single transducer to "paint" over the patient's belly. Employed experimentally at first, the value of the information it produced was immediately obvious. Today, almost all pregnant patients get a dating ultrasound at 12 weeks and at least one follow-up at around 20 weeks. Gestational dating is just one of its uses. Ultrasound can detect fetal anomalies long before birth, allowing obstetricians to prepare for them in advance or even correct them *in utero*.

It was long known that changes in the fetal heart rate could signal trouble. A healthy fetus has a heart rate between 120 and 160 beats per minute. It varies according to sleep and fetal activity. Rates persistently over 160 or under 120 are signs of fetal distress. The fetal heart can be auscultated with a stethoscope applied to the mother's abdomen, but that's impossible to do throughout a typical 18-hour labor. The answer to this problem was the fetal monitor, introduced at MCV when I was a fourth year student.

Just as ultrasound, these first monitors were primitive. A belt held a transducer over the fetal heart. The rate was continuously recorded on paper, something like a seismograph recording earth tremors, just as the monitors of today. The difference was in the measurement of uterine contractions. A saline-filled catheter in the uterus was connected to a twitchy, error-prone device that required constant adjustment. As part of my fetal monitoring elective, I spent uncounted hours at bedside, one eye on the monitor, the other reading Thackeray's *Barry Lyndon*. At that time, little was known about the meaning of the data the monitor produced. It was universally agreed that a heart rate between 120 and 160 was good. But what about the deviations that now turned up with practically every laboring patient?

Of special concern were decelerations. From time to time, rates could drop as low as 80 beats per minute. Remaining at that level was clearly a sign of fetal distress, demanding immediate delivery. And delivery was almost always by emergency Caesarean section. But often the rate would go back to normal. Obstetricians are, by and large, action-oriented doctors. It was hard to sit watching a monitor tracing alarming dips and do nothing. Without a body of knowledge to help interpret these ominous tracings, many C-sections produced healthy, screaming babies. Today, after more than 40 years of study and experience, the interpretation of fetal monitor tracings has become a science. What was previously thought to be dangerous is now known to be normal, and obstetricians are not as hasty with the scalpel.

In the 1970s, vaginal deliveries at MCV were done in two ways. Primigravidas were delivered with forceps over spinal anesthesia. Multigravidas delivered spontaneously, and forceps were used only occasionally. Patients labored mostly without medication, and they were most likely alone. There were no private birthing rooms. All patients labored together in a common area. Father, family, and friends were not allowed in.

Those having their first baby were taken to the delivery room when the fetal head had descended in the birth canal to a level where it could be safely grasped with obstetrical forceps. The delivering resident injected local anesthetic between the vertebrae into the spinal fluid — a practice unthinkable today, when all anesthesia is administered by an Anesthesiologist or Nurse Anesthetist. This 'spinal block' eliminated all feeling below the waist. As a result, the patient couldn't push. The resident slipped outlet forceps, which were curved to fit the pelvis, around the fetal head and literally pulled the baby out.

Sure, it sounds brutal, but that's how we were taught, and it worked fine. Sometimes, special straight forceps were used to rotate the head if it was fixed in a transverse position, a procedure obsolete today. Now, any arrest of descent is treated by Caesarean section. Residents of my day became quite skilled at forceps delivery. We were trained by an elderly professor who had learned forceps delivery at a time before antibiotics, when C-sections often resulted in infections that could be life-threatening. Forceps delivery was much safer. He knew all the techniques now relegated to the obstetrical dustbin.

Multigravidas were allowed to push until the head was just visible, or crowning, then were taken to the delivery room. Most delivered spontaneously. Injections of local anesthesia in the vagina provided limited anesthesia if an episiotomy was needed.

Epidural anesthesia changed everything.

A catheter inserted between the lumbar vertebrae and into the space above the membrane covering of the spinal cord — the dura — allows small amount of local anesthetic to be administered continuously. Epidural anesthesia can be started when the patient is in labor, eliminating most contraction pains. The mother still has enough sensation to allow her to push. Consequently, most vaginal deliveries today are spontaneous. In my last years of practice, I seldom had occasion to use forceps, usually only when my patient was too exhausted to push.

In the 1970s, only a few private patients received epidural anesthesia. Now, of course, it is the standard of care. Patients no longer labor together in a common area. Instead, they labor and give birth in private rooms, where they deliver in bed instead of on an operating table. The baby's father and her friends are allowed beside her from start to finish.

Tom Peters was one of the professors who specialized in obstetrics. In his 30s, he was close enough in age to relate with the residents. A friendly and likable fellow, he often hung out in the L&D resident's room. I'm sure he owned more than one suit, but I never saw him in anything but the same old brown one. Worn day in and day out, it had acquired a certain aroma. As the SAR in charge of West Hospital Labor and Delivery, I arrived one morning to find a medical student asleep in the lower bunk. He had a shoe over his face. "Hey, guy," I said, shaking him awake. "What's with the shoe?"

"I was up most of the night," he replied. "When I finally got a chance to get some sleep, Dr. Peters was in the top bunk."

Enough said.

First
Caesarean Section

Holding the scalpel like a pencil, my index finger resting lightly just above the blade, I made one rapid continuous stroke from navel to pubis. There was only the slightest resistance. I was a little surprised; this was the first big incision I had ever made. Maybe, subconsciously, I expected it to feel like cutting into a steak.

"Good," Dr. Peters said. "Now extend the incision along the same line down to the fascia." He was the assistant surgeon for my first Caesarean section. The fascia exposed, he went on: "Use Mayo scissors to open it vertically." That revealed the peritoneum — the filmy membrane lining the belly cavity. Incising the peritoneum, I exposed the pregnant uterus, swollen to the size of a basketball.

As a junior resident, I had assisted on many C-sections. Now I was an Assistant Resident. This was my first operative delivery as chief surgeon. At MCV, Caesareans were done with the patient asleep under general anesthesia. Speed was of essence, as it was important to deliver the fetus before it absorbed too much of the anesthetic drugs. Consequently, we operated through a midline incision. Today, except for the most extreme emergencies, almost all sections are done through a transverse incision above the pubis. It is more cosmetic than the midline cut, but definitely slower. However, with epidural anesthesia, speed of delivery is not a factor. Since there aren't any drugs in the patient's bloodstream, the fetus isn't depressed. Surgery can proceed at a slower pace, which allows more attention to detail and less blood loss.

"OK," Peters went on. "Open the uterus transversely, just above the bladder. Watch out for the uterine arteries running down each side."

The intact bag of water bulged through the opening. Amniotic fluid gushed out as I ruptured the membranes. I could see the fetus. She was lying on her right side. Only the trunk and left arm were visible, and her head was tightly wedged deep in the pelvis.

"Slide your hand between the pubic arch and the head," Peters instructed. "Then pull the head up into the incision."

My hand was a tight fit. I tugged on the head, but it wouldn't move.

"It's not coming!" I exclaimed.

"Push deeper — get the tips of your fingers over the crown and try again."

As the head began to move, suction tried to pull it back. Finally, it emerged with a squelch like a cow pulling her foot out of the mud. I clamped and cut the cord, and then I slipped my hand between the uterine wall and placenta to deliver the afterbirth. I closed the incision in layers while the newborn howled in the warmer.

"Very good, Doug," Dr. Peters remarked. "You can have another resident assist with your next one. You won't need me."

I was on top of the world.

Bones

In 1977, Seattle Slew won the Kentucky Derby, discos were the in-thing, people were dancing the Hustle, *Star Wars* was released, and I was the Senior Resident in charge of the East Hospital. One day, when nothing much was happening in the ER, I was handed a yellow registration form for a waiting patient. The complaint was "bones in vagina." Ordinarily, I assigned a junior resident to evaluate incoming patients, but this promised to be an amusing break from routine.

"I'll handle this one," I announced.

The patient was a scrawny woman in her 40s; but with her leathery seamed face, frowsy red-dyed hair, and smoke-cured voice, she could have passed for 60. Her breasts sagged beneath a tight tank top. She was wearing satin shorts and spike-heeled shoes — a hooker who had seen better days. Balled up in her fist was a nasty-looking wad of toilet paper.

"So," I said, "what seems to be the problem?"

"I've got bones coming out of my vagina," she replied.

"Bones. In your vagina."

"Yes, bones. Here, look."

She unwrapped the blood-stained tissue to reveal a few tiny bones. They looked like they came from a Cornish Hen.

"You say these were in your vagina? When did you first notice them?"

"Just this morning, when I finished with ... a client."

"OK, then. Let's take a look. The nurse will take you to an examining room and help you get undressed." I turned to the JAR beside me. "This ought to be interesting. She's obviously stuffed some chicken bones up there. Maybe we're going to need a psych consult."

Starting my exam, the first thing I noticed was that her breasts were black and blue with bruises and covered with puncture marks.

"What happened to your breasts?"

"That's where I inject Talwin."

Talwin is a synthetic narcotic, at that time sold on the street and used by addicts when heroin wasn't available.

"Why do you inject Talwin into your breasts?" I asked.

"Because I can't find any more veins."

OK, I thought, not my problem. With her feet in the stirrups, I moved on to the pelvic exam. As soon as I put in a speculum, I could see numerous small bones filling her vagina. Obviously a nut case, just as I thought. But clearing out the tangle, I could see that the cervix was open and filled with more tiny bones. They were coming from inside the uterus. Something way out of the ordinary was definitely going on.

"Call upstairs to the OR nurses," I ordered the JAR. "Tell them to get ready for a D&C."

With the patient under general anesthesia, I used long grasping forceps to clean out the vagina and explore inside the uterus. I retrieved most of a fetal skeleton, including a good-sized portion of skull. Now, these bones were as clean and white as any skeleton that had been lying under the desert sun for a year. Their size was consistent with a 16-week pregnancy. Probing higher, I could feel something soft still inside. Using a suction curette, I emptied the uterus of a small but unquestionably living placenta.

Later that day, I visited her on the ward.

"It looks like you tried to perform your own abortion," I said.

"No, I've never been pregnant."

"Come on, tell me the truth. I'm not going to get you in trouble. Just tell me what happened. Somebody botched an abortion."

"I wasn't pregnant and I didn't do anything. Bones just started coming out of me."

She never would admit to an abortion. Putting the clues together, I think she or someone else attempted a street abortion with a coat hanger. The bag of water ruptured without stimulating labor. The fetus died but the placenta survived, preventing labor while the fetus slowly dissolved. It is not uncommon for a fetus to be retained after intrauterine death. Even after a few days or weeks later, the body is still intact. How long, I asked myself, would it take for a fetus to turn to bare bones? And what kind of discharge would she have had during that time?

Her clients must not have been too choosy.

Hysterectomies Above and Below

Juanita Lopez had fibroids — balls of benign connective tissue that range from the size of a BB to the size of a cantaloupe. Hers were huge, and they made her belly the size of a woman 30 weeks pregnant. She had arrived at the Outreach Gyn Clinic in Tappahannock, Virginia, complaining of vaginal bleeding.

Senior residents spent part of their year on clinic rotation, traveling to obstetrical and gynecology facilities around the city of Richmond and as far out in the county as the Northern Neck. We were paid a small stipend. It wasn't much, but at last I was earning at least something. Less important than the money was the opportunity to scrounge up potential patients. I was one of four senior residents, and there were only so many cases needing surgery. I kept a notebook listing potential surgical patients. I wrote down the name and phone number of any patient I saw whose problems were not critical but would eventually require an operation. I called them when it was my turn to be senior resident on the Gyn rotation. Ms. Lopez was on my list.

"Hello, Ms. Lopez." I said to her over the phone. "It's Dr. Heritage. How are you doing?"

"About the same, Doctor. My periods are still heavy and there's some bleeding in between."

"Do you remember what we talked about last month? The bleeding and heavy periods are caused by the fibroid tumors in your uterus. Remember, I said they weren't dangerous — they aren't a form of cancer. But you don't have to put up with the bleeding if you don't want to."

"You mean an operation."

"That's right. I can either remove the fibroid and leave the uterus, so you can get pregnant again, or take the uterus out completely — a hysterectomy."

"Doctor, I'm 38 years old and I have four children. I don't want any more. But if you do this hysterectomy, will I go through the change?"

"Not at all. Women go through the change of life when their ovaries stop making estrogen. There's no reason to remove your ovaries. They'll keep on making hormones. You'll go through menopause normally, when you're in your 40s or 50s."

"OK then, let's do the surgery."

I admitted Ms. Lopez later that week and took her to the OR the next day. As a senior resident, I had assisted on, and performed enough, abdominal hysterectomies to do this one myself with only an AR as my assistant. Because of the size of the uterus, the surgery had to be done from above with an abdominal incision. A vaginal hysterectomy from below wasn't feasible. The uterus with fibroids was too big to fit through the vagina. She required an abdominal hysterectomy.

An abdominal hysterectomy is pretty straightforward. The connections of the ovaries and Fallopian tubes are clamped, tied, and cut. A series of pedicles are taken down each side of the uterus to the level of the cervix. The vagina is opened and the uterus, along with the cervix, is removed in one piece. The top of the vagina is closed, leaving it something like the toe of a sock. Then the abdominal incision is sutured, a dressing is applied, and that's it. With experience, the whole thing takes about an hour and a quarter. Ms. Lopez did fine post-operatively and went home a week later, her problems cured.

Ms. Anderson was next on my list. She was suffering with terrible menstrual cramps. My first thought was that she had endometriosis — endometrial tissue growing in the belly cavity, causing pain and scarring. But when I did a laparoscopy, the pelvis was free of any implants. A follow-up MRI revealed adenomyosis.

On the phone again: "Hello, Ms. Anderson. Heritage here. I think I can explain your menstrual pain. The MRI exam shows that you have adenomyosis."

"I never heard of that. I thought you were looking for endometriosis."

"Actually, adenomyosis is a limited form of endometriosis," I explained. "Instead of the endometrium growing outside the uterus, in the pelvis, it penetrates *into the muscle* of the uterus. Otherwise, it acts exactly the same. When you have a period and bleed externally, it bleeds between the muscle fibers, causing pain. And it gets worse with every menstrual period, just like endometriosis."

"So what do we do about it?"

"If you want to have more children, it can be treated with medications, but I believe your tubes are tied."

"Yes, they are."

"Well, it's a benign condition and nobody dies from it. The bottom line is you don't *have* to do anything. But if you want, the cure is a hysterectomy."

"My sister had a hysterectomy. She says her sex life went downhill afterwards."

"That happens, but it's because of other factors. The uterus has nothing to do with sexual pleasure; that comes from nerves in the vagina and the clitoris. Many women's sex lives actually improve after a hysterectomy, if they have adenomyosis. Remember how painful your pelvic exams were?"

"I sure do!"

"That's because your uterus is tender. Any pressure on the cervix, with intercourse or a pelvic exam, causes pain."

"Actually, my husband and I have given up sex. It just hurt too much."

"Why don't you and your husband talk things over and give me a call if you want to go ahead with surgery."

She called a few days later to schedule, and I did a vaginal hysterectomy the next week.

Because Ms. Anderson's uterus wasn't enlarged, it could be removed without the need for an abdominal incision — a hysterectomy from below. The operation is basically the same as the abdominal approach, but in reverse. The vagina is opened as the first step instead of the last, and so forth. Without the incision in the belly to heal, the patient recovers faster and can be discharged sooner. Ms. Anderson's surgery went by the book. Six weeks later, she was able to have intercourse without pain.

About that time, Dr. Leo Dunning, the OB-GYN Department Chairman, had scheduled a vaginal hysterectomy. Dr. Dunning was an eminent, nationally-recognized gynecologic cancer surgeon. That kind of surgery is always done through an abdominal incision in order to explore the rest of the pelvic cavity. He seldom performed vaginal surgery. An AR and I were assisting him during one of his rarely-performed vaginal hysterectomies for benign disease when we realized that his skills at the vaginal approach had grown rusty over the years. He had barely started, and the surgical field already looked like the dog's dinner.

"Well, fellows," he admitted, somewhat shamefaced. "I guess I'm making a mess of this!"

"Oh, no, Dr. Dunning," we chimed in unison. "You're doing just fine!"

A certain amount of discretion was called for.

Harry Berdann

As a senior resident, I had gathered the ARs and JARs under me on the Gyn rotation to meet with Dr. Harold Berdann, the new visiting professor from South Africa.

"Please call me Harry," he said in his euphonious Afrikaans accent — a mellow blend of British and Dutch. "I'm a senior consultant at a teaching hospital in Johannesburg. It is now my privilege to take a position as visiting professor at MCV. Why don't we go around the table and introduce ourselves?"

Dr. Berdann was in his 50s, his features pure Caucasian and his skin the color of someone who had spent his life ranching in Arizona. This was 1978, and apartheid was the state policy in South Africa. Under this system, Harry Berdann, whose ancestry included both blacks and whites, was officially deemed "colored." He was to become my mentor during my last year of residency. We shared a common interest in endometriosis, a benign but painfully crippling disease of women. We operated together whenever possible. I admired his surgical skills and urbane way with patients. A cultured man, he loved books and appreciated fine wine. We became good friends.

A month or so later, Debbie and I invited him to dinner at our home. At that time, I was greatly influenced by a book entitled *The Game of Wine*. Its theme was to match each course of a formal dinner with the appropriate wine, from appetizer to dessert. Debbie and I had given several of these "great dinners" for our friends and were now pleased to invite Harry Berdann. Under the mellow influence of several glasses of fine wine, the conversation turned to South Africa.

"Harry," I said, "I understand there's a lot of mineral wealth in your country. I've read about De Beers and the diamond mines."

"Quite right, Doug," said Dr. Berdann. "And De Beers still controls vast tracts of territory. There are places where, as you drive down the road, you can see nothing but acres of concrete bordered by razor-wire fences."

"Why is that?"

"Because you can quite literally dip your hand into the earth and scoop up fistfuls of semi-precious stones. De Beers doesn't want you doing that."

A few days after that evening, I visited Dr. Berdan in his office.

"Hello, Harry," I said as I took a seat. "You asked me to drop by."

"Yes, Doug. I have a question that perhaps you can help me with."

"Sure, Harry, if I can."

"You will recall that, at dinner, I mentioned that I don't plan to return to South Africa. That poses certain problems. My family is wealthy — we own a chain of liquor stores — but my limited exit visa only allowed me to bring 100 rand out of the country."

"Gee, Harry! That doesn't sound like much."

In fact, it equaled about $50.

"Of course, I have my salary as a visiting professor," he continued, "but that will not be sufficient for a permanent stay. So before we left, my wife and I took certain steps to assure an adequate income in the States. We swallowed diamonds. Which brings me to my question: where does one go to sell a diamond here?"

"I'm just a poor resident," I said. "I don't know anything about diamonds. How big a stone is it?"

"About five carats," he said modestly.

"In that case, I can help. I have no idea what a stone that size is worth, but it has to be a lot! You need to go to the center of the diamond trade. Take a taxi to the airport and get the next flight to New York."

I never found out how successful he was with his diamond transactions. Harry left MCV at the end of the year to take a position with a medical school in the Northeast. We corresponded briefly but soon fell out of touch. Many years later, I met another OB-GYN from South Africa at a medical conference. He knew Harry Berdann casually but hadn't seen him for some time. He told me that after apartheid ended, Harry had gone home.

Curse and Abuse

It was late in my last year as a resident. My old Toyota had developed the annoying habit of stalling when stopped on a hill. When it knocked off, it seemed to take forever to get the engine going again. As a senior resident, I was allowed to park in the same garage used by the faculty. Unfortunately, the garage was at the bottom of a steep hill. The road leading to it exited onto Marshal Street in downtown Richmond, a major thoroughfare during rush hour.

My shift ended at five. It had been a really tiresome day. Still dressed in my whites, I climbed into my car and slowly started up the hill. Traffic on Marshal Street was bumper to bumper. Cars ahead of me on the hill were moving slowly, but they were moving. Approaching the crest of the hill, I prayed that I could make the turn without stopping. If I stalled at the top, I would block the long stream of cars behind me. A campus cop was directing traffic at the intersection. The car just ahead of me turned onto Marshal and edged ahead, leaving just enough space for me as well. But just as I started to make my turn, the cop held up her hand gesturing me to stop. It was either go ahead or stall. I went ahead. Now safely on Marshal Street, I could see her speaking into her radio. Traffic continued to creep along.

Within a minute, a second campus cop appeared at my window. "Pull over," he ordered.

"Officer, you don't understand," I tried to explain. "I saw the other officer motioning me to stop, but if I did, my car would have stalled and really tied up traffic. Actually, there was plenty of space for me to pull out safely."

"I said, pull over!"

Marshal Street was a two lane road without any shoulders.

"Where do you want me to pull over?" I asked. "There's no place to pull over!"

"Stop the car and get out!"

I was getting angry. My father, grandfather, and great-grandfather were all notorious for their short fuses, and I am not one to suffer fools gladly.

"If I stop the car here in the middle of the street, it'll tie up the whole rush hour!"

"Get out of the car!" the campus cop screamed at me through the driver's window.

"OK, here I come, you mother-f#!*ing son of a bitch!" I yelled back as I threw the door open.

"Officer in distress! I need police backup!" he shouted into his radio.

Richmond city police were on the scene in moments.

"What's going on here," one of them asked.

"I tried to explain to him," I said, pointing at the campus cop, "that I didn't obey the officer directing traffic because, if I had, it would have caused a traffic jam. And then he comes along and tells me to stop my car and get out in the middle of Marshal Street!"

The police asked a few more questions and sized up the situation.

"Listen, Doc," said one of the officers. "I hear what you're saying, but you should have followed directions. Remember that in the future."

They were going to let me go.

"I want him arrested!" shouted the campus cop.

"On what charge?" I demanded.

"Curse and abuse!"

There was a discussion out of my hearing between the police and my nemesis, the campus cop. When they were finished, one of the police officers approached me.

"Doc, he insists on pressing charges. Sorry, but we gotta take you into the station."

I was bundled into the back of a squad car, taken to the local Richmond police station, and put in a holding cell. After a short while, I was allowed to see a magistrate.

"Why are you here, Doctor?" he said, eyeing my whites.

"It all started with my lousy car," I began.

I told him the whole story.

"Well," the magistrate said, "it seems the campus policeman has insisted on pressing charges. I have no choice but to set a court date. In the meantime, you're free to go on your own recognizance."

"Thank you, sir. Could you please set my appearance for the first thing in the morning? I have patients to take care of."

"That won't be a problem."

A few days later, I appeared in Richmond District Court. The day's docket was posted beside the courtroom door. At the top was "Douglas Heritage — Curse and Abuse," followed by various miscreants with charges like "breaking and entering" and "felonious assault." The courtroom was packed with spectators — there had to be over a hundred people in there. I rose when the judge made his entrance. He seemed like a good-humored man in his early 40s. The campus cop, serving as plaintiff and witness, stood beside me.

"Doctor, it seems you are charged with curse and abuse," the judge began. "Would you please tell the court what this is all about?"

I told my story again, explaining what had happened.

"I'm very sorry that I called the officer a bad name," I concluded. "I thought he was being unreasonable, but I shouldn't have let my temper get away from me."

"The doctor has apologized and seems remorseful," the judge announced. "I'm going to dismiss this case."

"But your honor!" the cop shouted. "You can't just let him go! He called me a mother-f#!*ing son of a bitch!"

The overflowing courtroom exploded in raucous laughter. The judge's face went through several contortions as he tried not to laugh.

"Nevertheless, officer, I'm going to let the doctor go."

I turned to face the cop and gave him a big grin before walking out.

Board Certification

*I*t is extremely important for physicians to be certified by the medical board which oversees their specialty. Almost all hospitals require that a doctor requesting privileges be either board certified or board eligible. Any physician who has completed a recognized residency program is deemed board eligible, but to become board certified requires much more.

The certification process for the American Board of Obstetrics and Gynecology has three parts. First, pass a written exam. Second, practice for two years and maintain detailed case files on each patient. Third, present those files to the board examiners and pass a grueling oral exam. Only after satisfactorily completing all three parts is one awarded the coveted certification.

The written exam is taken at the completion of the residency program. It includes questions on anatomy, physiology, biochemistry, pathology, and endocrinology, as well as anything related to clinical practice. I studied for hours every night while the Watergate scandal played out on TV. At first, I couldn't believe Nixon was a crook. This was the man who got me an "A" in German Literature! My opinion changed when the tapes were released.

After weeks of preparation, I still felt there was more to memorize. Theoretical questions like, "What is the precursor steroid of estradiol?" would pop into my head and send me rushing back to the textbooks. In fact, I had over-prepared.

All senior residents took the test together in one of the Sanger Hall classrooms. It was multiple choice, fill in the correct circle with a number two pencil, just like the PSAT and SAT in high school and the MCAT (Medical College Aptitude Test) as a senior undergraduate. We were allowed three hours to complete it, but the questions looked too easy, and I wasted time studying each one for a trap. As time went by, my fellow residents began to hand in their answer sheets and leave. I still had pages to go. I began to panic. I had never run out of time with any of those other tests. Finally, I was the only one left in the auditorium with a lot of questions still unanswered when the proctor called an end. I was devastated! I was sure I had failed. But I must have been almost 100 percent right on the questions I *did* answer, because I passed. There was no grade — just pass or fail. I might have passed with the equivalent of a "D," but I passed.

That was in 1978. For the rest of that year, I practiced with an established OB-GYN group in Petersburg, Virginia, then left in 1979 to start a solo practice in Woodbridge, Virginia. In both locations, I had plenty of patients and scrupulously maintained my case files in preparation for the oral exam.

The American Board of Obstetrics and Gynecology oral exams were held each year in Chicago. I flew there on the eve of the 1980 presidential election. Jimmy Carter was running for a second term, opposed by Ronald Reagan. I checked into the hotel where the exam was given and spent the rest of that day and night going over my cases and quizzing myself with potential questions. The next morning, all the candidates formed a long line as we waited to be assigned to our examiners.

After what seemed like forever, I met my examiners — two eminent professors. They played good cop, bad cop roles. I didn't know the kindly good cop, but the bad cop's name was famous; I recognized him as the author of a notable textbook. He was especially hard on me. Years later, I spoke with him at a medical conference. He was jovial and friendly and quite surprised when I told him he had scared the crap out of me as an oral examiner.

After they finished with me, I was turned over to a third examiner to be questioned on histology and pathology. I was given a set of slides to view through a microscope and quizzed about each one. Then I was grilled by the first two examiners, who had reviewed my case files. Finally, it was over. I was dismissed without any comment. Results would be mailed in a few days.

Reagan had won the election before my flight home had landed. As a Republican, I took his victory to be a good omen. And it was. I passed. I was board certified!

~ PART 4 ~

Private Practice

Katie

*I*n 1985, Debbie and I saw The Cars perform live at Merriweather Post Pavilion in Maryland; they opened with "My Best Friend's Girl." Ronald Reagan was inaugurated to his second term. Madonna launched her career as a pop star. Our daughter, Barbara, was six. And Debbie and I had grown apart.

Debbie was never happy after we moved from Petersburg. Houses in northern Virginia were shockingly expensive. Our new house was barely adequate and not nearly as nice as the old one. I was in the midst of my career as a solo OB-GYN with a brand-new office and a growing patient clientele. Debbie — driven as always by her hard-wired, farm-family work ethic — vacillated between homemaking and her career. She was never happy. At home with Barbara, she was bored. I encouraged her to take a job with a Northern Virginia cytogenetics firm, but she quit after a few months over an argument about the methods they used, simply because they were different from the ones she had been taught. Now, with Barbara in day care, Debbie was alone all day with nothing to occupy her time. I suggested she join a Women's Club. She seemed to enjoy it at first. Then her driven nature kicked in. She volunteered to head every project and then complained to me about all the work being heaped on her. Soon, it was the end of the Women's Club and off to a new job. The work-home cycle went on and on, with Debbie increasingly miserable with each repetition. I found it impossible to live with a perpetually unhappy companion. We separated in 1985.

I rented a townhouse one mile from my hospital and lived alone for two years. Katie and I met casually at a party. After exchanging the usual banal conversation, the subject of the supernatural came up. We discovered that we both had a life-long love of horror, both in books and film. We ignored the other guests and spent an hour swapping "Did you read…?" and "Did you see…?" Our friends laugh when we say "horror brought us together." I made sure to get her phone number.

Katie is blonde and tall and has beautiful blue eyes. Not the stereotype "dumb blonde," she had graduated from college with an English degree and was going to law school when we met. On our first date, we went to see a re-enactment of a Civil War battle at New Market in Virginia's beautiful Shenandoah Valley. I had a deli pack a picnic basket. We drove there in my five-liter Mustang with the top off. We watched the battle while sitting on the grass and sipping German wine. Then it was back to Woodbridge for dinner and off to a club for dancing. I was hooked! My divorce was finalized in 1987. We got married the same year. After our honeymoon in England, Katie and I settled into life together — not always easy. But we got things sorted out as we grew accustomed to each other.

For the first five years, we lived in a townhouse. Barbara visited every other weekend and stayed over for two weeks in the summer. She and Katie got along great. Being so much younger than me, Katie was more like a big sister than a stepmother. Life was good. My practice was thriving. Soon it was time to move to a nicer house. In 1992, we bought an eight-acre lot halfway between Woodbridge and Manassas. And since Katie and I always loved the mansions featured so often in mysteries and horror movies, we designed and built a large Tudor house and decorated it with tapestries and swords hanging on oak paneling. We live there still.

Katie used her law degree as a credential to enter public administration. Starting in a low-level job in the Fauquier County criminal justice system, she advanced rapidly. A master of politics, socially adept, and charming, she is now the Deputy County Administrator. And she plays a wicked game of backgammon.

Katie is the best thing that ever happened to me. I am married to my best friend.

Eclampsia

"Eclamptic coming in!" shouted the paramedic as the door to Labor and Delivery crashed open. A woman was strapped to the gurney, her back and legs rigid, her body bucking, her jaws clamped on a rubber bit.

"Call her doctor," a nurse yelled as she and two others rushed to the patient's side.

I was the only obstetrician in L&D that day. It was my responsibility to deal with this emergency until her regular OB arrived.

"Five grams of magnesium stat!" I ordered. "Maintain two grams an hour."

"We called Dr. Tyler," the clerk said. "She'll need an hour to get here."

The patient and her baby didn't have an hour.

Eclampsia is the most critical disease of late pregnancy. It starts with a condition known as pre-eclampsia. For reasons still unclear, on occasion a pregnant mother's kidneys start to malfunction in the third trimester. She begins to spill protein in her urine — proteinuria — and her blood pressure goes up. As long as there are less than five grams of protein in the urine and her blood pressure is less than 110 diastolic or 160 systolic, she is considered a mild pre-eclamptic. Mild pre-eclampsia is treated with medication, bed rest, and careful observation. Provided fetal testing shows no signs of distress, these patients are usually delivered at or near term. Most obstetricians see several cases of mild pre-eclampsia every year.

Severe pre-eclampsia is another matter entirely. When the limits defining the mild form are exceeded, both the fetus and mother are at serious risk. Red blood cells start to break down, and platelets — essential to clotting — fall to disastrously low levels, leading to uncontrollable hemorrhage. The liver is damaged, compounding the problem. The patient is also at risk for placental abruption, a premature separation of the placenta from the uterus, depriving the fetus of oxygen. If not delivered immediately, the mother may start to seize, which can lead to both fetal and maternal death. This is the condition known as eclampsia.

"The seizures have stopped," the nurse observed. "The five grams of mag are in, and the two grams are running."

IV magnesium depresses nervous activity. It's the gold standard for treating both severe pre-eclampsia and eclampsia. The patient was in a coma but wasn't convulsing anymore.

"What's the fetal heart rate?"

"It's 95, Doctor," the nurse replied.

Normal fetal heart rate is between 110 to 160 beats per minute. This baby was in serious trouble.

"Has Anesthesia been called?"

"They're on their way, Doctor."

"All right, we need to do a C-section ASAP! Make sure Neonatology is standing by." A nurse rapidly inserted a Foley catheter into the patient's bladder and we rolled her to the operating room. "No time for an epidural," I told the anesthesiologist. "Fetal distress. You gotta put her to sleep."

It typically takes 15 or 20 minutes to start an epidural and have it take effect. This baby didn't have 15 or 20 minutes to spare. General anesthesia takes less than a minute.

We heaved her onto the operating table. The nurses slopped Betadine on her belly as Anesthesia began the induction. After the briefest of scrubs and gowning in haste, I stood by her side, scalpel in hand, waiting for her to go under.

"Say when," I said to Anesthesia.

"Go ahead," he replied.

I made one stroke from navel to pubis and a second to expose the uterus. I laid open the uterus from top to bottom. Typically, C-sections were done with a cosmetic transverse incision just above the pubis and the uterus opened just above the bladder. But that takes time, and time was something this baby didn't have. This was a classical C-section — the fastest way to deliver.

I pulled the infant out and passed her to the neonatologist. There was no cry, no motion. I had done all I could do.

"How's is she?" I asked Neo with a sinking feeling as I began to repair the incision. I could hear the puffing of the Ambu bag ventilating the baby's lungs. Had we been too late? Then, a faint cry! Soon it was the full-throated scream of a healthy newborn.

I pulled my gown off my sweat-soaked scrubs and spoke to the mother, "She's going to be fine!"

Dr. Tyler arrived and took over the postpartum care. She told me later that the patient recovered without any problems and went home with her new little girl a few days later.

Infertility

Mrs. Caroline Su desperately wanted to have a baby.

"My husband and I have been trying ever since we got married in Korea," she said. "I was an army brat. We met in Seoul and fell in love right away. It's important for him to have children, most especially a boy. I don't know what the problem is! My two sisters both have kids."

"How long have you been having sex without contraception, Carol?"

"Two years now."

"Are your periods regular?"

"Not really. Sometimes I'll go a couple of months without having one. It's been that way ever since I started."

"OK, that gives me some ideas."

Female infertility is a complicated issue which affects roughly 10 percent of partnerships in the United States. The most common causes are hormonal in nature, especially failure to ovulate on a regular basis. The next most frequently encountered cause is damage to the Fallopian tubes that prevents the egg and sperm from meeting. Such damage may be caused by sexually transmitted infections, like gonorrhea and chlamydia, or adhesions from previous surgery. I could eliminate adhesions as a likely cause, since Mrs. Su didn't have a history of abdominal surgery. Her irregular periods were the clue to the problem.

"Carol, before we go any further, you need to understand that investigating and treating infertility is difficult and often not successful. If we're going to proceed, you have to accept that fact and be willing to follow my instructions exactly."

"Yes, Doctor. I can do that."

"Great! So on to the easy part. Much of the time the problem is with the man. Your work-up is going to involve a lot of tests and office visits. For him, we only need one test — a sperm count. If it's normal, we go on with you; if abnormal, he will need to see an Urologist for treatment." I gave her a request for Mr. Su to have the test. "Now, until we get his results back, we can start a simple, but very important, program for you. I don't think that you are ovulating on a regular basis — that's why your periods are irregular. We call it anovulation. To find out, I'm going to have you keep a temperature chart."

"How will that help?"

"When you release an egg, your resting temperature — what we call your basal body temperature — goes up by a few tenths of a degree. By charting your basal temperature, I can tell if and when you are ovulating. The thing is, the temperature rise is too small to register on a regular fever thermometer. You'll need to get a special basal body thermometer. Any drugstore has them. And most important, you have to take your temperature first thing in the morning, before you get out of bed. Any activity, even getting up to go to the bathroom, will mask the small rise I'm looking for."

I showed her how to fill out a temperature chart and mark the days when she had her period and those when she had intercourse. A month later, she was back. Her chart didn't show an ovulation peak.

"Carol," I said. "It looks like you haven't ovulated, just as I suspected. Mr. Su's sperm count was normal, so I think failure to ovulate on a regular basis is the problem. But before I start any treatment, let's check it for another month."

The next month, the chart was the same. It was enough evidence to start treatment.

"I'm giving you a prescription for Clomid," I said. "You take one pill a day for five days, starting on day five of your next menstrual period. Hopefully, that will make you ovulate. Here's the best dates to have intercourse." I marked her basal body temperature chart. "If you don't have a period by day 32, you might be pregnant, you might not have ovulated on this dose, or you might have ovulated and didn't conceive for some other reason.

So call me if your period starts or you are late. Either way, I will need to see you."

Caroline Su had to make several visits and changes in medication, but eventually her pregnancy test was positive. I had the great pleasure of delivering her boy nine months later.

Gretchen VanHorn's case was different. She had a history of clockwork menstrual periods and had delivered a healthy girl before she had surgery to remove a ruptured appendix. Since then, she had been unable to conceive.

I discussed my approach with her: "Mrs. VanHorn, I suspect your problem is a blockage in one or both of your Fallopian tubes. Were you quite sick when your appendix ruptured?"

"Very much so. The doctors said I had peritonitis — my whole belly was infected. I was on IV antibiotics for several days after the surgery."

"When the lining of the abdomen — the peritoneum — is infected, it produces scar tissue we call adhesions. They may be blocking your tubes. I'm ordering an HSG – a hysterosalpingo-gram. It's a kind of X-ray. By injecting dye into the uterus and watching it fill the tubes, I can determine where the blockage is.

The X-ray showed both tubes to be blocked in their middle.

Today, the treatment of choice for tubal occlusion is in-vitro fertilization (IVF) or the "test tube baby." But this was 1988. At that time, IVF was still new and not widely available. The only means of opening the tubes was by surgery. I reviewed the HSG findings with the patient.

"Both of your tubes are blocked," I said, "almost surely due to adhesions. If you want, I can operate and try to open them up. But I can't make any guarantee of success. I might not be able to clear the blockage, and even if I do, they may close up again. All I can tell you is that I have had special training in this procedure and been successful several times in the past, resulting in healthy babies."

"Thank you, Dr. Heritage. I need to discuss this with my husband."

"Of course. Call me if you want to go ahead."

She called a few weeks later to schedule the surgery.

Tubal reconstruction, now made obsolete by IVF, was state of the art at that time. I had spent a week at Mt. Sinai in Cleveland taking a special course on microsurgery. The professors there were world-famous tubal surgeons. One of them maintained a clinic entirely devoted to infertility surgery. He had patients from as far away as India. I learned to operate under a microscope, using needles smaller than an eyelash and sutures thinner than a human hair. Using these techniques, I removed the blockage in Gretchen VanHorn's Fallopian tubes. Six weeks later, a repeat HSG showed them to be open. She went on to have two more children.

Gretchen was one of my last microsurgery patients, which I regretted. I really enjoyed the fine, detailed work it required. I continued to treat anovulation as before, often with success, but over time I did less and less infertility work. Like so much else in the field of Obstetrics and Gynecology, what used to be the province of the local OBG has been taken over by subspecialty groups.

Most of these patients are now referred to Infertility Clinics with the capability to do IVF.

But I still had the joy of doing the delivery.

Two Patients with Twins

Like most obstetricians, I occasionally had patients with twin pregnancies, which isn't surprising, as 30 of every 1,000 live births in the United States are of multiple gestation. Of twins, two-thirds are fraternal and one-third identical. When I was a resident, the proper way to deliver twins was still in dispute. The problem was the second fetus: if it was in breech presentation, there was a chance the head might be too big to pass through the pelvis and be trapped during a vaginal delivery. The result would be disastrous. Old-school obstetricians, trained when C-sections were dangerous, favored delivering the first twin vaginally and then reaching into the uterus, grasping the feet, and turning the baby head first — internal podalic version.

It's another maneuver now confined to the OB trash bin. Today, if the second twin is breech, a Caesarean section is the standard of care.

Juanita Ortiz was pregnant for the second time. Her first baby had been delivered vaginally without problem and weighed over eight pounds. This time she was carrying twins, confirmed by her first ultrasound at 12 weeks. We discussed how that would affect delivery:

"First of all, Juanita, I don't want you to worry. Chances are both of your babies will be fine. We'll just have to take some special care."

"What kind of care, Doctor?"

"Nothing unpleasant. The most common problem with twins is premature delivery, usually a few weeks before your due date. But babies born as early as a month before do well. I'll need to see you in the office more frequently than routine, and we'll get an ultrasound every four weeks."

"My sister had twins and had to have a Caesarean section. Will I need one too?"

"Hopefully, no. It depends on the position of the second fetus. If it's head down, there should be no problem with a vaginal delivery. Otherwise, most obstetricians agree that a C-section is the safer way to go."

"When will I know?"

"Not until the end. The babies shift position all through the pregnancy. During the last third, I'll order an ultrasound every week or two. If both are head down, you can go into labor naturally. Even so, I'll get a final scan in Labor and Delivery to make sure number two hasn't changed position."

Eight months later she was in labor. The last office ultrasound showed the second twin to be vertex, but the first was breech. A bedside scan in L&D confirmed the presentation to be unchanged. This posed a dilemma.

"Juanita," I said, "the second baby is still head down, but the first is coming as a breech. Many would recommend a C-section, and nobody could fault them for it. But your first child was large and delivered without a problem. I believe I can deliver your first twin vaginally as well as the second. It involves a certain amount of risk, but you avoid an operation. It's your decision."

"Have you done these breech deliveries before, Doctor?"

"Yes, and without any problems. But that's just history; I can't make any promises."

"Then let's go natural."

We took Juanita to a combined operating and delivery room when I could feel the baby's bottom through the bag of water. Twins can't be safely delivered in a birthing room. The nurses rolled in two fetal monitors and applied transducers to record the fetal heartbeats. With her feet in stirrups and the Neonatology Intensive Care team standing by, I ruptured Baby A's amnion and grasped the fetal bottom. With the patient pushing, the body slid out. I put a finger in the baby's mouth to flex the head and pulled gently on the legs to easily complete the delivery. With the newborn boy passed to Neo, I broke the second bag of water and applied a scalp electrode to Baby B's head. The heart rate was normal. Now it was a matter of waiting. After about five minutes, uterine contractions started up again. With only a few pushes, Juanita delivered a girl without a problem. Both babies were screaming their heads off in their warmers.

"You hear that, Juanita?" I said as I delivered the placentas. "You have a little boy and a little girl! They're both doing fine!"

"Thank you so much, Doctor Heritage!"

Not all twin deliveries go as planned. Amy Lovell's twins were consistently vertex-vertex by serial ultrasounds, perfect for vaginal delivery. I didn't expect any problems. I gave her the usual instructions and followed her closely. All was normal until week 36, when Mrs. Lovell's blood pressure registered 150 over 95. A dipstick urine test showed 2+ protein.

"Amy," I said, "it looks like you are developing a condition we call pre-eclampsia. It's pretty common and usually responds to bed rest. But with your twins, we can't be too careful. I want to admit you for some blood tests and another scan."

She went into the hospital that afternoon. I got a phone call at 11:30 p.m. the same night.

"Dr. Heritage," said Sandy, the night nurse, "I'm sorry to wake you, but you ought to know. I have Mrs. Lovell in ante-partum. Her blood pressure has been 160 over 105 for the last two readings."

"OK, send her to L&D. I'm on my way. Tell them to get a stat bedside ultrasound."

When I arrived, her pressure was about the same. After a quick exam and a few reassuring words with the patient, I checked the admission lab results that had just been completed at 9 p.m. They were all consistent with pre-eclampsia except for one outlier. Her liver enzymes were sky-high. This rang a little bell … something in a med school lecture … something about late pregnancy and the liver.

I went to the hospital medical library and pulled out Catesby & Ratcliffe's *Comprehensive Obstetrics*. Flipping through the index, I found "Fatty liver of pregnancy, 532-538."

I skimmed through the paragraphs: "… occurs once in 15,000 pregnancies … up to 85 percent fetal and maternal mortality … associated with symptoms of pre-eclampsia … hallmark is a significant elevation of liver enzymes."

That was it! She didn't have pre-eclampsia. She had a fatty liver disease, and there was a real chance that she and her twins might die.

Back at her bedside, I studied the two fetal monitor strips. Both showed a mixed pattern — not enough to demand immediate action but far from reassuring. My digital exam showed the cervix to be long, closed, and firm. Induction of labor was not an option.

"Amy," I said, "I know we planned on a vaginal delivery. But you have developed a dangerous condition involving your liver. The only cure is immediate delivery. And that means a C-section."

"Can't you make me go into labor? I know there are medicines that start contractions."

"Amy, this is your first pregnancy. We know that a first labor typically lasts 18 hours, even when labor starts by itself. And an induction, given that your cervix isn't ready, would take even longer. I don't think you and your twins have that much time."

She gently ran her hand over her stomach and let out a small sigh. "OK, Dr. Heritage. Whatever is best for my babies. Let's do the C-section." She wasn't concerned for herself.

The twins, both girls, had mild prematurity complications that fully resolved after a few days. Her recovery was a little rocky, but with the help of internists I consulted, she made a full recovery.

It was a humbling experience. So much of obstetrics is repetitive — vaginal deliveries, frequently-seen complications, and routine Caesarean sections — that I felt I knew it all. It was a blow to my ego to realize that wasn't the case — that no matter how rare, how unlikely, serious problems can arise that I knew nothing about.

Thank God for the medical library!

French Girl

"What can I do for you?" I asked the petite young lady sitting across from my desk. Her name was Marie. According to my new patient form her age was 22. She was quite attractive, with that reddish-gold hair known as Titian blonde. She had a nice smile and her pert nose tipped up just a trifle. Not much younger than my daughter, I felt comfortable thinking of her as a "girl," even if that wasn't politically correct.

"I just need a routine exam and birth control before I return to France," she replied.

"Have you been in the States long?"

"Only a few months. I had to do some research at the University of Virginia."

"Really? What kind of research?"

"I am working on a doctorate degree in medieval studies. UVA has some books and documents in their rare book library that I needed to consult. Now I am off to Paris and back to the Bibliotheque Nationale."

"That sounds really interesting. I've always enjoyed reading history, especially about the middle ages. Now, you said you want birth control …"

Routine questions followed — past health, allergies, and so forth. That done, it was time for her physical exam. With all new patients, I required a complete head to toe exam, naturally with an emphasis on the breasts and pelvis. I called my medical assistant.

"This is Shannon," I said. "She'll help you get ready."

Shannon conducted her to an exam room.

"Please take off everything in the changing room. I'll leave a cape and sheet on the exam table for you," she said. (What she didn't say was that the cape covers the torso and the sheet goes in the lap.) "I'll be back with the doctor in a few minutes."

A few minutes passed. I stepped into the exam room. Marie was sitting on the exam table completely and utterly naked! Politely, I turned my head away, which was really hard to do, as even my brief glance had revealed a stunning figure to match her lovely face.

Shannon, embarrassed by the patient's brazen nudity, rushed past me. Snatching up the cape, she admonished, "The cape goes on like this, open in the back. The sheet covers your legs!"

Marie was puzzled.

"But why?" she asked. "He is going to see everything any-way! This is the way we do it in France."

"That may be, but in America, our patients are more mod-est. They like to be covered up," I replied, thinking that being a gynecologist in France certainly had its benefits.

Shoulder Dystocia

❧

"Push, Janet! Push!" urged the nurses. "We can just start to see the baby's head!"

This was my second delivery for Janet, an attractive young woman in her early 30s. Her first pregnancy had gone by the book, ending with the spontaneous vaginal delivery of a healthy girl. This pregnancy had been normal as well. Based on the ultrasounds, she was expecting a boy. The first stage of labor, from onset of regular contractions to full dilation of the cervix, had lasted a typical 12 hours. She had received an epidural as soon as active labor was confirmed and was comfortable. Delivery was close now. The second stage of labor, from full dilation to delivery of the newborn, was almost at an end. I had no reason to expect anything but another easy delivery.

"The head is crowning! Get ready, Doctor!"

I slipped on my gown, gloves, and face shield and waited at the foot of the bed, towel in hand. There didn't seem to be a need for an episiotomy.

"Here he comes!"

The head emerged from the vaginal opening, face down as normal. I applied pressure to Janet's perineum with the towel to help it stretch and prevent lacerations. Then the baby's head pulled part way back in.

"Uh, oh. Turtle sign!" exclaimed Tammy, one of the best of the L&D nurses. Like a startled turtle pulling its head back into its shell, a baby's head will pull back when its shoulders are too broad to fit through the pelvic outlet. This critical complication of labor is called shoulder dystocia. When the fetal head is caught like this, it compresses the umbilical cord. Blood flow from the placenta to the fetus is dangerously reduced or even blocked completely. There are, at best, five minutes to get the baby delivered before it expires of asphyxiation. And you can't just pull the baby out with forceps. Too much traction will tear the nerves in the fetal armpit, resulting in Erb's palsy — the affected arm will be paralyzed for life.

"OK, give me full flexion of the legs and suprapubic pressure," I ordered.

By pulling a patient's legs back against her chest as far as possible, the pelvic opening is slightly enlarged. Simultaneously pressing down just over the pubic bone, a McRoberts maneuver, usually results in delivery. I had used these methods before to successfully deliver many cases of minor shoulder dystocia. But now, with Janet, the baby's head remained stuck in place.

"We have major shoulder dystocia. Call a crash team!" I shouted.

This emergency demanded immediate assistance. As we waited for the team of OB nurses, Neonatology specialists, and Anesthesiology to arrive, Tammy crawled onto the bed in order to press with all her weight over the pubis. I cut an episiotomy to enlarge the vaginal opening. About a minute had gone by. There was no progress.

"OK," I said. "I'm going to try Woods' screw."

The baby's shoulders were trapped cross-wise. There is more vertical space in the bony pelvis than transverse space. The idea is to grasp the fetal head and rotate the shoulders to the vertical plane. If McRoberts fails, this almost always works. But not this time. I tried rotating left, then right, but the baby wouldn't budge. Two minutes had elapsed. My scrub clothes were soaked with sweat.

"I'll try to deliver an arm. If that fails, we'll have to do a Zavanelli and go to C-section. Get the room ready."

I had read about the Zavanelli maneuver but, thankfully, had never performed or witnessed the dangerous procedure. A C-section can't be done with the fetus partially delivered and its oxygen cut off. The baby would be dead before the first incision. Dr. Zavanelli reported a case in which he had, as a last resort, flexed the baby's head and forced it back into the vagina, then

rushed to Caesarean section. According to the obstetrical literature, this had occasionally been successful.

"I'm going for an arm." I forced my hand into the vagina
and past the fetal head. I could feel the baby's arm tucked up beside his chest. Three minutes had passed. Hooking a finger into
the crook of his elbow, I slowly drew the arm out, trying to avoid
a fracture. With the arm delivered, the shoulders slumped into a
vertical position and the baby slid out immediately.

He wasn't breathing.

"Let me have him!" the Neonatologist snapped.

Clamping and cutting the umbilical cord as fast as possible,
I passed him over. Had I been in time? I could hear frantic activity at the incubator as I began to repair the damage caused by the
traumatic delivery. There were vaginal lacerations to be sutured
as well as the large episiotomy.

"OK, we have a steady heartbeat and he's breathing on his
own. I think he's going to be OK," the Neonatologist said with
relief. "We'll take him to the NICU [neonatal intensive care unit]
for observation, but I think he's going to be OK."

"How's my baby?" Janet asked tearfully. She and her family
were, of course, terribly worried.

"You gave us quite a time," I answered, "and you needed
some extra stitches, but you're both going to be fine."

It's sometimes said that the practice of obstetrics is long
hours of boredom interspersed with occasional minutes of terror. Shoulder dystocia is at the top of the terrifying list. Without

a trained nursing team and a physician familiar with the proper maneuvers, the baby will almost always die.

Shoulder dystocia usually occurs when the fetus is atypically large. Big shoulders have a hard time passing through limited pelvic space. In an ideal world, these oversize babies would be detected before labor sets in and delivered safely by Caesarean section. Unfortunately, there are no satisfactory methods of accurately assessing fetal size. Prior to the introduction of ultrasound, an obstetrician's only tool was the laying on of hands. The size of the uterus — small, average, or large — for a particular gestational age was the only clue. It turns out that ultrasound is scarcely more accurate. It is not unusual for a C-section to be performed for what seems a very large fetus only to deliver an average-sized baby. To complicate matters further, shoulder dystocia also occurs with patients who seem to have a small or normal-sized fetus.

One group definitely at risk for this complication are pregnant diabetics. Poor maternal glucose control feeds extra sugar to the developing fetus, making for big babies. Pregnant diabetics need to be watched carefully and seriously consider a Caesarean if the fetus appears large at term.

Ovarian Cyst

*E*sther Harris was referred to me by the Emergency Room for evaluation of an ovarian cyst.

"Good afternoon, Ms. Harris," I said. "I see by your paperwork that you were in the ER last night for abdominal pain. A CT scan showed a cyst on the right ovary."

"Yes, Doctor. I was fine until yesterday when I started to have a pain in my belly."

"Did the pain come on suddenly, almost like a stroke of lightening?"

"That's right."

"Was the pain down low on the right side?"

246 MY LIFE AS AN OB-GYN: A Look Behind the Scenes

"Yes."

"And is it better now?"

"It still hurts a little, but not like last night."

"Did your last period start about four weeks ago?"

"Yes, it did. How did you know?"

"Ms. Harris, obviously I need to examine you, but as we sit here I am almost positive you have nothing to worry about. I believe you had a ruptured ovarian cyst."

Her story was classic, and a perfect example of wasted money, time, and medical resources. When a woman is diagnosed with an ovarian cyst, it can be pretty scary. Often, her first thought is ovarian cancer. Most don't understand that *all* women in the reproductive years form ovarian cysts with each menstrual cycle. That's how the ovary works. Immediately following the menstrual flow, the ovary starts to produce estrogen and begins to ripen an egg, which develops within a pea-sized *follicular* cyst. The egg matures in two weeks and is released when the small cyst ruptures, sometimes with a brief pain called *mittelschmertz* — literally "pain in the middle." The remains grow into a new *luteal* cyst. It starts to manufacture progesterone, preparing the lining of the uterus to accept a fertilized egg.

Luteal cysts are typically the size of a marble but occasionally are much larger. If the woman becomes pregnant, the cyst persists and continues to produce progesterone, which maintains the pregnancy. If the egg has not been fertilized, the luteal cyst shrinks and disappears, usually without any symptoms. This triggers the next menstrual cycle. But once in a while, the cyst ruptures painfully, with symptoms exactly like those of Ms. Harris: sudden onset of low, one-sided pelvic pain about four weeks after the last menses. The pain typically lasts about 24 hours and resolves spontaneously in two or three days.

Although this normal cycle of events is well documented, a visit to the Emergency Room almost invariably results in unnecessary blood work, an ultrasound, and sometimes a CT scan, all of which could have been avoided if the attending doctor had just asked the right questions. Unfortunately, medicine today is practiced with technology instead of reason. The fear of missing a rare diagnosis and the consequent lawsuit is a contributing factor. Asking the right questions, issuing a prescription for a mild painkiller, and encouraging the patient to follow-up if they aren't better in a few days saves a lot of time, trouble, and money.

During the course of my career, I saw patients with ruptured benign cysts at least once a month. After examining Ms. Harris to confirm my diagnosis, she left my office with a prescription for a mild analgesic and instructions to call in two days if she was still in pain. She never called.

A luteal cyst is termed "functional" because it occurs as a normal function of the reproductive system. There are other kinds of ovarian cysts — neoplastic, or "new growth" cysts — which are abnormal. They may be benign or malignant. Fortunately, the benign ones occur far more frequently than cancerous ones.

Both kinds may be asymptomatic. If large, they may be noted on a routine pelvic exam. Whenever an ovarian cyst is found and persists, it must be evaluated to rule out cancer. A blood test known as CA125 is usually elevated in the presence of cancer, but it may be above normal in the presence of benign conditions such as endometriosis. That said, an elevated CA125 raises the index of suspicion. The only sure way to rule out malignancy is to surgically remove the cyst, or even the entire ovary, for a pathologist to examine microscopically. If benign, nothing further need be done. Cancer, of course, demands further evaluation to determine its stage — the degree to which it has spread through the body — followed by further surgery and chemotherapy.

In many ways, medicine has advanced far beyond the imagination of the doctors that preceded me. An OBG in 1970, or before, had only his knowledge, experience, and physical examination to rely on when assessing an ovarian cyst. The technologies of today — ultrasound, CT scanning, MRI, laparoscopy, advanced blood tests — have certainly aided in saving many lives. But at the same time, they have become a crutch. Rare is the patient with abdominal pain who leaves the ER without an ultrasound, CT scan, and extensive blood work. Everything conceivable has been done to arrive at a diagnosis — except talking to her.

Thank God, I encountered only one case of ovarian cancer during my entire private practice. I will tell you about her — Mary Boyd — later on.

Ectopic Pregnancy

-1977-

I was the AR on duty in the East Hospital ER. Ms. Jefferson presented complaining of pain. I took her case.

"Are you pregnant?" I asked first off.

"I suppose so," she said. "My last period was 'bout two or three months ago. I did one of those home tests and it said I was."

"There's been no bleeding since then?"

"No."

"Where does it hurt?"

"Low down on my right side."

"How long has it been hurting you?"

"It started a few days ago but got a lot worse this morning."

On exam, she was very tender in the right lower quadrant, but I couldn't feel any mass. Checking an HCG (Human Chorionic Gonadotropin) level was the next step. This hormone is produced by the embryo and its level in the mother's blood correlates roughly with gestational age. For a pregnancy of eight to 10 weeks, her level should be around 230,000. Her value of 4,500 was strongly suggestive of an ectopic pregnancy. But if her pregnancy was earlier than I thought based on her last menstrual period, say six to eight weeks, that level would be normal. I explained my thinking to the patient.

"Ms. Jefferson, it's possible that you have a pregnancy in a Fallopian tube, or it may be that you have a perfectly normal early pregnancy. There's no way to be sure today. I want you to go home, rest, and come back in two days. I'll get another blood test then. If you start to have really bad pain, or bleeding from the vagina, come right back."

For a normal intrauterine pregnancy, HCG levels should double every 48 hours. Two days later, her value was 4,700. The pain was no better, perhaps a little bit worse.

"It looks pretty certain that you have a pregnancy in your Fallopian tube," I explained. "It's got to come out. If it continues to grow, eventually the tube will rupture and you can bleed to death."

"Does that mean an operation?"

"Yes, I'm afraid so. The only treatment is to remove the entire tube. As soon as possible, before it ruptures."

I admitted her for a laparotomy. I was chief surgeon with Dr. Peters assisting. Using the same 8-inch transverse incision as I would for a hysterectomy or Caesarean section, I located the right Fallopian tube. There was a slight bulge in the middle. Clamping and tying, I removed the entire tube and closed the incision. The patient went home after a week's stay in post-op.

-1987-

Now let's put Ms. Jefferson into an imaginary time machine and transport her forward 10 years. She arrives at my office with the same symptoms and HCG levels. I order an ultrasound, which shows an empty uterus and a 1-centimeter mass in the right Fallopian tube.

"Ms. Jefferson, it looks pretty certain that you have a pregnancy in your Fallopian tube," I explain. "It's got to come out. If it continues to grow, eventually the tube will rupture and you can bleed to death."

"Does that mean an operation?"

"Yes, I'm afraid so. But not a big one. I can use a laparoscope to visualize the tube and pass instruments through the scope to remove the pregnancy. The tube stays in place and may continue to function. It's an outpatient procedure. You can go home that afternoon with nothing more than a Band-Aid."

The operation the next day goes as planned. She goes home as scheduled.

-2007-

Now let's put her back into our time machine and fast-forward another 10 years. Ms. Jefferson comes to my office with the same symptoms and lab reports. An ultrasound shows a 1-centimeter mass in the right Fallopian tube and no evidence of an intrauterine pregnancy.

"Ms. Jefferson, it looks pretty certain that you have a pregnancy in your Fallopian tube," I explain. "It's got to come out. If it continues to grow, eventually the tube will rupture and you can bleed to death."

"Does that mean an operation?"

"No, not at all. I can treat you with methotrexate"

"What's that, Doctor?"

"It's a medicine originally used to treat cancer. It will kill the pregnancy in your tube and your body will absorb what remains. No surgery needed. I'll give you the first dose today, then I'll need to see you back in four days and a week later for repeat HCG testing. If the values are going down, we do nothing else. If not, I'll give you a second dose."

Her levels fell as expected, and six weeks after the first dose they were down to zero. Her treatment was finished.

Like many other things in obstetrics and gynecology, the diagnosis and treatment of ectopic pregnancy has changed radically since I was a resident. Conservative treatment for an intact tubal pregnancy is considered the standard of care. Today, the only indication for removing an entire Fallopian tube is rupture, or else the patient will bleed to death. And that, tragically, still occurs. Although ectopic pregnancy occurs in 1 to 2 percent of gestations, it causes 3 to 4 percent of pregnancy-related deaths, largely due to failure to seek timely medical care. The use of methotrexate has been a huge advance in the treatment of this condition. Unfortunately, it has limitations. The ectopic mass must be less than 3.5 centimeters in size, the HCG levels must be less than 5,000, the patient cannot have other serious problems (such as liver disease), and she must be reliable, as several follow-up visits are required. If those conditions cannot be met, the alternative is salpingostomy — laparoscopic removal of the pregnancy from the tube.

Dealing with ectopic pregnancy has come a long way since Dr. Garrigues, writing in *The Science and Art of Obstetrics* (1909), advocated the use of electricity: "As strong a current as the patient can bear without an anesthetic should be applied, the sitting should not be shorter than 10 minutes, and it ought to be repeated daily until all signs of pregnancy have disappeared."

Circumcision

"Do you want your baby circumcised?" I asked the new mother.

"Is it important for his health?" she replied.

"Not really. There may be a slight decrease in cancer of the penis, but it's mostly just a social custom. If Dad or the baby's brothers are circumcised, most parents decide to do it so their son will look the same. It's entirely up to you."

A circumcision is the removal of the penis' foreskin. At one time, almost all boys born in America were routinely circumcised. It has since fallen out of favor to a degree, especially with Hispanics. Nevertheless, I circumcised the majority of the babies I delivered. If the parents wanted it done, I would do it, but I never encouraged it.

The procedure is carried out during the first few days after delivery using one of three techniques. For Jews, it is a religious ritual performed by a *mohel* with a guillotine-like instrument. Another method uses a plastic bell tied on the head of the penis (the glans) until the foreskin drops off. I was trained with the Gomco instrument. A metal cup is placed between the glans and foreskin and clamped in place. The foreskin is cut free with a scalpel. Pressure from the clamp prevents any significant bleeding. The whole thing takes perhaps 5 minutes.

I was assigned to perform circumcisions as a third year student. "Circs," as they were commonly referred to, were considered "scut" work, along with starting IV's and drawing blood — procedures deemed beneath the dignity of the residents. They were more than happy to turn the job over to the students. I rapidly learned to hate the job. It was tedious and boring, and the fear of a mistake always lurked in the back of my mind. An urban myth circulated amongst the students on OB rotation. The story went that a student had once unwittingly applied the scalpel *below* the bell and cut off the glans. A mistake too horrible to contemplate! Nevertheless, I always tried to do a nice, neat job and was proud of my results.

"How many do you have today?" I asked the neonatal nurse.

"Twelve. I've lined up the instrument trays for you. Have fun," she snickered as she wheeled in the bassinets.

That was 30 years ago. Now, I had a circumcision to perform on my private patient's baby.

"I don't know," I said to the nurse as she removed the newborn's diaper to expose his penis. "That's just a stub!"

A circumcision requires the penis to be of a minimal size. Too big is rarely, if ever, a problem, but if it's too small, the Gomco won't fit properly. You can't put the foreskin back after you've cut it off, so in these cases, it is best for the little boy to grow a bit and have his circumcision done later as an out-patient.

"He's too small. Wrap him back up. I'll tell the parents."

The entire family on both the mother and father's side were visiting. My patient's room was crammed with brothers, sisters, aunts, uncles, and grandparents.

"I'm sorry," I began, "but I think it would be best to wait until he's a little older before he's circumcised."

"Why's that?" asked the new father.

"Well, his penis is just too small for the instrument. It would be dangerous to go ahead now. He'll be bigger in a few weeks. It can be done as an outpatient then."

"Too small you say? Why, he's just like his father!" shouted the new dad's mother, cackling with laughter.

I could feel my face turn red with embarrassment for the poor guy. What could I say?

"Well, in any case, he can go home with you today," I mumbled as I beat a hasty retreat.

Placental Abruption

"We need help!" shouted the young man as he elbowed open the door to Labor and Delivery. His other arm was supporting a very pregnant woman slumped between him and a female companion. "She's bleeding and it won't stop!"

I jumped up from the front desk as nurses hurried to assist. "What happened?" I asked as we helped the woman into a delivery room. From the size of her belly, she was clearly at term. Her thighs were drenched with blood. As the nurses undressed her, I went out to reception to get some answers.

"Who is she?" I asked. "And who are you?"

"She's our client," responded the man's companion, a drab woman in her 20s. She was wearing a shapeless sack of a dress and long strings of cheap beads around her neck. Her mousy brown hair was straight as a stick.

"That's right," added the man. His jeans were torn at the knee. A large wooden cross dangled across his work shirt. He appeared about the same age as his companion. "We're birth assistants. My name is Ted and this is Dawn." He gestured towards his companion. "We were assisting Megan with a home delivery. Everything was fine until she started to bleed. Dawn thought it was just 'show.'"

"We expected some bleeding," Dawn added. "After all, that's normal when the cervix starts to dilate. But then it got really heavy and Megan began to scream about the pain. We both prayed for her but it wouldn't stop."

"That's when we thought maybe she needed to go to the hospital," Ted added.

"So you called an ambulance?"

"Megan lives way out in the country. We figured it would take too long for an ambulance to get there, so we put her in our car."

"You two wait here. Don't go anywhere."

I went back to the delivery room.

"There's no fetal heartbeat with the doptone," Monica, one of the nurses, said. "Blood pressure is low — 100 over 65 — but seems stable. Pulse 110. We sent a stat CBC, blood group, and type."

They had an IV running.

"Call Radiology for a stat bedside ultrasound," I said. "Have the lab type and cross two units of packed cells. Did you do a pelvic exam?"

"No, Doctor. She might have a placenta previa."

"Absolutely right. The other possibility is placental abruption. Monica, ask those two out there if they did a vaginal exam at any time."

In the case of placenta previa, the afterbirth implants across the opening to the cervix and begins to bleed as the cervix dilates. If an examining finger punctures the placenta, it results in catastrophic uncontrollable hemorrhage, followed by both fetal and maternal death. In cases of serious bleeding at term, placenta previa must be ruled out before performing a vaginal exam.

"They say they didn't do any vaginal exams," Monica reported.

"OK, it's probably an abruption."

At this point, a radiology tech arrived with a portable ultrasound machine and began scanning.

"Term-size fetus," she reported, still scanning. "There's the heart. No heartbeat. Placenta is anterior and fundal. There's a large collection of blood between the placenta and uterine wall."

262 MY LIFE AS AN OB-GYN: A Look Behind the Scenes

"Thank you. That's all we need." I took the patient's hand and leaned over to speak softly. "Megan, I'm so very sorry, but your baby has passed away."

"No, no!" she sobbed. "Everything was fine! I was going to have a home birth, like my sister! She did OK! What did I do wrong?"

"You didn't do anything wrong. Sometimes bad things can happen, things you can't control. It's not your fault."

"My baby is dead?" It was part question and part plea that this was all a nightmare.

"Yes, I'm afraid so, Megan. Now we have to take care of you."

I turned to the nurse. She had attached a fetal monitor. The contractions were no more than moderate. The patient needed to be delivered as soon as possible but, as she was stable, there was no need for a Caesarean section. I decided to augment her labor to enable a vaginal delivery.

"Monica, start Pitocin at two milliunits a minute and increase every 15 minutes until we get good contractions. Give Megan 2 milligrams of morphine IV." That would control her pain and sedate her as well. "Let me know as soon as the lab results come back. I'm going to have a word with our 'birth assistants.'"

They were sitting in the lobby, exchanging fearful glances.

"How did you two meet Megan?" I asked.

"She answered our ad in the newspaper," Dawn replied.

"You placed an ad? How did you describe yourselves?"

"As birth assistants."

"Have either of you had any medical or midwife training?"

"Not exactly — nothing formal like in school," Ted answered, looking at his feet.

"So what made you think you were capable of assisting a woman in labor?"

"We read a lot of books. That's how we knew the bleeding was normal when it started. The books said it's called 'show' and it's normal. Anyway, women have been giving birth at home forever. It's delivery in a hospital that's unnatural, what with all the drugs and machines. We wanted everything to be natural."

"Megan's baby is dead. The placenta separated prematurely. There was no blood flow to the baby, no oxygen. It asphyxiated. If she had been in a hospital, attached to one of those 'unnatural' machines, we would have seen that happen with enough time to save the baby. That baby's death is on your heads. You two wait here. Don't go anywhere."

I left them in the lobby and called the police. I got a detective on the line and explained what had happened. "As far as I'm concerned, those two are guilty of criminal negligence, at least!" I said. I was furious.

By the time an officer arrived, the pair had disappeared. I spoke with the detective in person the next day.

"We tried to trace them with what little information we had," he said. "There's no fixed address. I know how you feel, Doctor, but there's nothing we can do."

Megan delivered a stillborn, but otherwise completely normal, boy. She was able to hold him for a few hours before he was taken away.

A stillbirth is one of the hardest things an obstetrician has to deal with. How do you tell a woman that her baby, who she has felt moving within her for months, is dead? A doctor with any degree of empathy shares her grief. It's a hundred times worse when the stillbirth could have been prevented. True, home birth has its adherents. Provided that it's supervised by a trained midwife with ready ambulance access to a nearby hospital, it's relatively safe. Women have delivered at home all through history. But take a walk through any cemetery dating to the 1800s or earlier. Read the gravestones. See how many belong to young women with an infant buried beside them. Throughout history, women lived in fear that their pregnancy would kill them. It was not until the 20th century that most deliveries took place in a hospital. The trouble is that labor and delivery can go from completely normal to catastrophically wrong in a heartbeat. When that happens, delivery in a hospital setting may make the difference between life and death.

Endometriosis

"Good morning, Ms. Washington. I'm Dr. Heritage."

"Good morning, Doctor."

Arnelia Washington was a new patient, a pleasant-appearing African-American woman in her mid-30s. She was dressed for work in a business suit and blouse.

"What can I do for you?" I queried.

"Doctor Heritage, I hardly know where to begin. My periods are all messed up. They hurt me so bad I can't go to work. And me and my husband have been trying to have a baby, but no luck."

"Have you consulted anyone about this?"

"Doctor, I been to the ER so many times I can't count 'em. They just tell me it's normal, women are supposed to have pain with their periods. Just take some Tylenol and rest. That's all they say. They don't care. Once they did a blood count and said I was anemic — told me to take an iron pill. Like an iron pill was gonna help my cramps! But the monthlies just keep getting worse and worse. Lately they aren't even monthlies. I bleed in between. Sometimes I bleed for two weeks and then it starts all over again."

"This pain with your periods — does it start when you begin to bleed or before?"

"It starts before."

"A few hours before?"

"No, like two weeks before, then it gets worse and worse."

"Is the pain all over your belly or mostly down low?"

"It's all down low. Sometimes it goes into my legs."

"Have you always had pain with your periods?"

"Ever since I started, I've had cramps, but nothing like now."

"Has the cramping been getting worse over time?"

"It was about the same until last year. Then it started getting worse and worse."

"You say you've been trying to get pregnant. I see on the registration form you've had one child."

"Yes, a little girl, when I was 28."

"How long have you been trying this time?"

"We started last year, so about nine months."

"How often do you have intercourse?"

"We used to do it two or three times a week, but lately hardly at all."

"Why is that?"

"Because it hurts so bad."

"Do you use pads or tampons?"

"I used to use tampons but now I use pads."

"Is that because it hurts to put in a tampon?"

"Yes."

"Ms. Washington, I'm glad you've come to see me. I'd like to do a quick exam, then we'll let you get dressed and talk some more here in my office. My assistant, Shannon, will help you get ready."

I was 98 percent sure what her problem was, and the pelvic exam confirmed my opinion. Her upper abdomen wasn't tender, but she complained of pain with light pressure above the pubic bone. On digital exam, the cervix was very sensitive. So were the uterus and both ovaries. There were no palpable masses, and the uterus was normal size.

Sitting together in my office, I explained my diagnosis. "I'm almost certain that you have endometriosis. You might as well have a signboard around your neck with the diagnosis."

"What's endometriosis, Doctor?"

"First of all, it's a benign condition and in no way life threatening. Sometimes the lining of the uterus, the endometrium, begins to grow within the abdominal cavity, where it doesn't belong. When you have a menstrual period, it bleeds internally, which is very irritating to the surrounding organs. Have you ever had a splinter?"

"Of course."

"Imagine lots of little splinters low in your belly. The endometrium growing inside inflames normal tissues. The body reacts by feeling pain. Every time you have a period, it's bleeding internally and getting worse with every cycle."

"That explains why my menstrual cramping is getting worse."

"Exactly. Ordinary cramping, the kind most women have to some degree, begins when the period starts, or a little before. The first clue to endometriosis is cramping that begins days or weeks before you bleed. That's when the endometrium starts to grow, in the second half of your cycle."

"What about the long periods and bleeding in between? Does it cause that, too?"

"It's often related, but abnormal bleeding can have other causes as well. That's something we have to look into."

"And the pain with intercourse?"

"Sure. You remember how painful that exam we just did was."

"Do I ever!"

"Your cervix, uterus and ovaries are very tender. Anything that touches or moves them — intercourse, inserting a tampon, a digital exam — will cause pain. And endometriosis can cause infertility. There are many other reasons, of course, but it's high on my list in your case."

"If that's what I have, how do you treat it?"

"First, I have to be 100 percent sure that's the problem, and the only way to be sure is to see it and take a biopsy. No X-ray, ultrasound, or MRI will pick it up. If you want to go ahead, we need to do a laparoscopy."

"What's that?"

"With you asleep, I insert a telescope — called a laparo-scope — through a tiny incision in the navel. If I see implants of endometrium, I'll take a biopsy. At the same time, I can also use a laser through the laparoscope to destroy them. Over the years, I've had a lot of patients with this disease. I've done a lot of laparoscopy. Some were completely cured, some had to follow up with medicine."

"What about the bleeding?"

"Good point. At the same time, I'll look into the uterus with a different, smaller, telescope called a hysteroscope. If the bleeding is caused by a fibroid, I can remove it at the same time."

"Well, Dr. Heritage, you've explained all this pretty well. I can't go on without doing something. I think I'll have the surgery."

I did the surgery two weeks later. She had several endometrial implants on the ovaries and pelvic wall, which I vaporized with the laser. There were also a few adhesions to the right ovary, which I cut with laparoscopic scissors. The uterine cavity was free of fibroids and the D&C specimen was benign. Four weeks later, she was back for a post-op check.

"How are you doing?" I asked.

"Doctor, I feel so much better. I had a period last week. There was a little cramping, but some ibuprofen took care of it. That awful nagging pain is gone! And my period lasted just four days and wasn't heavy. Thank you for helping me."

"It was my pleasure. If you still want a baby, go ahead and start trying. Otherwise, let's see you back in six months."

It didn't take six months. Nine weeks later, she returned to confirm a normal pregnancy and start prenatal care.

Endometriosis, though not life-threatening, can be crippling. The incidence of this disease is poorly understood. Studies have shown that it's present in six percent of women undergoing tubal sterilization, though they have no symptoms. The incidence may be as high as 50 percent in teenagers suffering severely painful periods. The trouble is that it can't be diagnosed by blood tests, ultrasound, or CT scanning. It remains one of the few areas left in medicine where a physician's experience trumps high tech. Asking the right questions, as I did with Ms. Washington, can create a high index of suspicion, but the only way to be sure is to see implants with the human eye. Many women have never heard of this disease. Many of them are passed over as cranks or hypochondriacs by health care providers without the time or knowledge to ask those questions.

When I was a resident, endometriosis was thought to be a disease limited to women in their 30s and 40s. This was because, at that time, the only way to verify it was by doing a laparotomy — completely opening the belly as one would for a hysterectomy. Therefore, the disease wasn't severe enough to convince a surgeon to operate unless it had been growing from adolescence. With the advent of laparoscopy, endometriosis has been diagnosed in women of all reproductive ages. Personally, my youngest patient with biopsy-proven endometriosis was 12 years old.

Abnormal PAP

Janet Miller would have been attractive if not for her nose, which was much too large for her narrow face. She was back in my office for a colposcopy, and she was confused.

"Dr. Heritage, on the phone you said I had an abnormal PAP smear. Does that mean I have cancer?"

"No, Janet, not at all. The PAP we did last week shows some abnormal cells, but nothing like cancer."

"But still, it's not normal."

"No, it's not. That's why I asked you to make an appointment for colposcopy. You see, nobody goes to sleep healthy and wakes up with cancer of the cervix. It takes months, probably years, to develop."

"So, if I don't have cancer, what *do* I have?"

"Cervical dysplasia. It's a pre-cancerous transformation of the cells covering the cervix — the epithelium. The earliest change is called mild dysplasia. If left alone, over time it may advance by stages to moderate, then severe, dysplasia. There can even be cancer limited just to the surface epithelium — carcinoma in situ. All of these conditions can be easily cured. It's only when the surface cancer penetrates into the body of the cervix that it becomes life-threatening."

"OK, I guess I feel a little bit better."

"Great. Now, today I'm going to look at your cervix with a colposcope. It's a kind of binoculars with a short focal length. Dysplasia causes certain changes to the surface which I can see with magnification. I'll take one or two small biopsies, no bigger than a match head, from any areas that look questionable. Depending on what the laboratory report says, I can choose the easiest way to get rid of the problem."

Janet's biopsy showed moderate dysplasia. I treated her in my office with cryotherapy. Freezing the surface of the cervix kills the epithelium, just as frostbite kills toes. New normal tissue rapidly grows back in its place. Eight weeks later, a follow-up PAP smear was normal.

Another of my patients, Ms. Garcia, had a more advanced problem. Her colposcopic biopsy showed severe dysplasia. Being closer to a cancerous change, it can't be treated by freezing. It must be physically removed with surgery — an operation known as cervical conization. In a hospital operating room, with the patient under either local or general anesthesia, the cervix is incised around the abnormality and a plug of tissue shaped like a cone is removed. When I was a resident, we were taught to do this with a scalpel. In my private practice, I used a high-power CO2 laser instead of a knife. The laser cauterizes blood vessels as it cuts, resulting in less blood loss. Ms. Garcia's outpatient operation went by the book. Eight weeks later, her cervix was completely healed and her PAP smear was normal.

For years, the origin of dysplasia was a mystery. It is now well documented that it starts with infection by Human Papilloma Virus. There are dozens of strains of HPV. A few cause genital warts, which are unsightly but benign. Some other strains cause dysplasia and, if untreated, cervical cancer. Tragically, almost 13,000 cases of cervical cancer are diagnosed each year in the United States, and over 4,000 die. They are dying of a completely preventable disease. If every woman had a PAP smear on a regular basis, the precursor — dysplasia — would be detected long before the condition became potentially fatal.

HPV infection is transmitted by genital contact. As sexually activity starts at earlier and earlier ages, so too does the incidence of HPV infection and dysplasia in teens and young women. In 2006, a vaccine against the HPV virus was introduced. It protects against 70 percent of the strains causing cervical cancer and 90 percent of those causing genital warts. I wholeheartedly agree with the recommendation that girls and young women from ages nine to 26 be vaccinated.

No woman looks forward to her visit with the gynecologist. But that visit, along with regular PAP smears, may save her life.

German Girl

My new patient was not cast in the Hollywood stereotype of a German girl. She was a brunette, not a blonde, and her eyes were brown instead of blue. But she spoke with a heavy accent.

"Doctor, I am sorry my English is not so good."

I glanced at her name on the registration form and replied, "Gisela — may I call you Gisela? I'm sure your English is better than my German."

"*Vielleicht* [Perhaps]. But it is very bad. Do you speak any German?"

"*Ja, aber ich kann nur eine bischen Deutsch sprechen.* [Yes, but I can speak only a little German]. Let's try English."

I did my best to elicit a meaningful history, but her English was, indeed, limited. All she could tell me was that she had a pain in the belly. I decided to proceed with a physical exam and only ask questions that seemed pertinent. My medical assistant, Shannon, led her to an exam room and showed her how to get undressed.

Her temperature, pulse, and blood pressure were all normal, most likely excluding any major problem. Gently palpating her abdomen, I couldn't feel any masses. She was slightly tender in the left lower quadrant — the location of the lower bowel. Perhaps the problem was nothing more than constipation.

"Have you had a bowel movement?" I asked.

"I am sorry, I don't understand."

"Have you been to the bathroom?" I forgot the 'going to the bathroom' is a pure Americanism for having a bowel movement. The euphemism is usually not understood by Europeans, who wonder why you are asking when they last had a bath. She obviously didn't know what I meant.

Sometimes, a language difficulty can be overcome with mutually understood gestures, like putting a hand to mouth means "eat." But I couldn't think of any that would help with this question. And I certainly didn't know the German words for "bowel movement." As a last resort, I resorted to my pidgin German: "*Haben Sie gemachte Scheise?* [Have you made shit?]" I can't recall when I learned the word *scheise*, but it sure wasn't in German Literature class.

"JA!" she exclaimed, her face a blazing crimson. The diagnosis of constipation seemed to be eliminated.

I decided she most likely had a benign functional ovarian cyst, which would resolve itself in a few days without treatment. I tried my best to explain my diagnosis and gave her a prescription for a mild painkiller. Without another word, she leaped off the exam table, snatched up her clothes, threw them on, and rushed out the door.

Mary Boyd

❦

"I'm sorry, Mr. Boyd," I said to the man seated in the visitors' surgical waiting room. "We couldn't get all of it."

Mary Boyd had ovarian cancer. A schoolteacher in her early 40s, she had come to me a month earlier with a number of vague complaints: a feeling of pelvic pressure, bloating, fatigue, and occasional nausea, all of which can be symptoms of benign conditions.

"How long have you had these problems?" I asked as we sat in my office to take a new-patient history.

"I don't know," she responded. "For several months at least. I thought it was just constipation — maybe that's all it is — but laxatives don't seem to help. And I'm so tired lately. It's been keeping me from going to work. That's when I decided to see somebody."

The rest of her history was unremarkable: married, two children after normal pregnancies, no past surgery or major medical issues. There was a good chance there wasn't any gynecological problem at all. A referral to a gastroenterologist would be the next step if her exam was normal.

"OK, Mrs. Boyd. I need to do an exam. My medical assistant, Shannon, will help you get ready."

Starting with a chest exam, I noted that both of her breasts were rock-hard. On pelvic exam, there was a non-tender mass in the region of the left ovary. The uterus was fixed in place and immoveable.

"Go ahead and get dressed, Mrs. Boyd," I said. "We'll talk some more in my office."

"What do you think's going on?" she asked apprehensively.

"You have a mass in the area of the left ovary, possibly a tumor of the ovary itself. Hopefully, it's benign. We need more information. I'm ordering a CT scan of your pelvis and abdomen, some more or less general X-rays, and some blood work. Try not to worry. I'll call you as soon as I get the results."

One of the blood tests would be a CA125, a marker for ovarian cancer. I decided not to mention the abnormal breast findings. She already had enough to worry about.

"OK, Doctor. Whatever you think is best."

A week later the results were in. The CT scan showed a 6-centimeter left ovarian mass and what appeared to be normal lymph nodes. A chest X-ray revealed fluid in the pleural cavity between the lungs and chest wall. Both breasts were infiltrated with abnor-mal-appearing tissue. The CA125 was significantly elevated.

"Mrs. Boyd, I'm sorry, but the tests so far indicate cancer, probably ovarian. The chest X-ray also indicated that it may have spread to your breasts and chest cavity."

"I see." She was taking this awful news with extraordinary calm. "What now?"

"I'd like to refer you to an internist who specializes in diseas-es of the lungs — a pulmonologist. He'll probably tap some of the fluid in your chest — a thoracentesis — to check for cancer cells."

"What then?"

"There are a number of options. Let's see what the pulmon-ologist finds, and then we'll go over them."

A week later the results of the thoracentesis were back — positive for malignancy. We met again in my office.

"There's no doubt now that you have ovarian cancer and it has spread to your chest and probably your breasts," I said. "You are going to need chemotherapy and possibly radiation treatment — that will be up to an oncologist to recommend. What you need to decide is whether or not to have a hysterectomy."

"If the cancer has spread, like you say, what would be the point?"

"It's called debulking. Because the tumor in the ovary is large, it's unlikely that chemotherapy or radiation would have much effect. By removing the bulk of the cancer, the odds are improved in your favor. Against that is the surgery itself, with the risks involved, like bleeding or infection, as well as the recovery."

"What do you recommend?"

"I have to tell you that, even with surgery, your chances are not good. Every individual is unique, of course, but the overall five year survival rate with this type of cancer is probably no better than 17 percent."

"Seventeen percent for five years."

"I'm afraid so."

"In that case, Dr. Heritage, I'll have the surgery."

I expected that this would be a difficult operation, so I asked a general surgeon, John Maggio, to assist me. I had worked successfully with John on a number of previous cases. It was important to have a surgeon on board who could deal with other organs, such as the bowel, that might be involved.

Mrs. Boyd's operation took place the next week. Opening the abdomen revealed a cancerous ovary the size of a lemon adherent to the uterus and pelvic walls. There appeared to be no other spread of malignancy. Our hopes began to rise. The hysterectomy with bilateral salpingo-oophorectomy (removal of both ovaries and Fallopian tubes) proceeded in a textbook fashion. But with the uterus and ovaries removed, we could then see the previously concealed rectum and sigmoid colon. They were heavily involved with cancerous growth. Extremely disappointed, we paused to consider how to proceed.

"John," I said, "you could remove this portion of the bowel, but would it be the right thing to do for her? She has stage four cancer with metastases to the chest and breasts. I don't think it would improve her chances of survival. She only has a few weeks, maybe a month, left. It would mean spending her last days with a colostomy."

"I agree," he replied. "There's no point in it. "

So we closed the incision without proceeding further. While the nurses were applying a dressing, I went out to the waiting room to speak with her husband.

"I'm sorry, Mr. Boyd," I said. "We couldn't get all of it."

He looked up from the magazine he had been studying. "So what now?" he asked calmly.

I was taken aback. It was as if I had told him that we couldn't remove a hangnail.

"Well, she needs to spend a few days in the hospital and then recover at home. I'll arrange a referral to an oncologist to get her started on chemotherapy."

"OK, Doctor. Thank you for helping."

Again, this weird indifference to terrible news. I returned to the recovery room wondering what was going on. Her husband seemed to be of at least normal intelligence — surely he realized that I had just pronounced a death sentence. Maybe he felt that God would heal her, but I had never heard anything from either of them to suggest religious belief. The next day, I visited Mary during my morning rounds. Post-op, she was doing fine:

no fever, her incision looked good, and she was taking liquids without difficulty.

"Mary, I'm very sorry, but we couldn't remove it all without taking out a large part of your bowel. That would have meant a colostomy. We didn't think you would want that."

"No, I wouldn't. So how long do I have left, Doctor?"

"I'm sure that, with chemotherapy, it could be several months."

"Several months. With chemotherapy. Well, that's that, then." She seemed as indifferent to this awful prognosis as her husband had been. Her recovery proceeded uneventfully, and she was discharged to home on schedule. I saw her back for her initial post-op exam four weeks later. During that time she had seen an oncologist and received the first dose of chemotherapy. A vaginal exam showed the cuff — the top of the vagina sewn shut when the uterus is removed — to be slightly open.

"Mary, you're doing well," I said. "Remember, no heavy lifting for a few more weeks, and stay on schedule with the chemo."

"No, I don't think I'm going to do that. The first dose made me as sick as a dog."

"But it's very important! Remember, I had to leave some of the cancer behind. You really need the chemo."

"No, I don't. I hate feeling sick. I'm done with it."

"That's your decision to make, as long as you understand the risks." I wasn't going to hector her about a therapy I knew wouldn't make much difference. "I'm a little concerned about the vaginal incision. Let's see you back in two weeks."

Two weeks later the vaginal cuff had sprouted an ugly purple and gray cauliflower the size of a ping pong ball.

"Mary, the cancer is progressing. You really need to get back on the chemotherapy."

"No, thank you, Doctor," she said indifferently. Two weeks later, the cancer in the vagina had shrunk. Two weeks after that, the vaginal cuff was clean. A chest X-ray showed less fluid in the thoracic cavity and a decreased density to the breasts. At six months, all tests showed her to be free of cancer.

I have no explanation for the miraculous recovery of Mary Boyd. It is truly the most remarkable medical encounter I have ever had. Since then, I have informally discussed her case with several GYN cancer specialists at medical seminars. All agree that one dose of chemotherapy could not have made a difference. Maybe she had faith that God would intervene, but she never mentioned any such beliefs to me or my staff. Personally, I think that by accepting her fate and refusing to give in to fear, she freed herself from stress. Stress is well known to impair the immune system, which tracks down and destroys cancer cells. She allowed that system to heal her. Much later, I heard that after 10 years the cancer finally recurred and she passed away. But Mary Boyd, by her will alone, gave herself 10 good years of life.

Time to Quit

By the end of 2014, I had been in private practice for 36 years, all but one in Woodbridge, Virginia. Over that time, I had delivered thousands of babies and performed just about every kind of major and minor gynecologic surgery. I was close to many of my patients. Some, who had moved away, continued under my care, driving from North Carolina and West Virginia for routine yearly exams. Though not an actual grandfather — my daughter, Barbara, hasn't had a child yet — I felt like one. I was now delivering babies for those girls who I had delivered decades earlier. I ran my practice like a family and took good care of my three employees. My personal office was also my man cave. My desk faced a large bust of Augustus Caesar, photos of Stradivari and Guarneri violins adorned the walls, and my bookcase was filled with non-fiction of all sorts, as well as textbooks. For many years, I was quite comfortable with my practice.

Then medicine started to change, and not for the better. The late '90s saw an effort to control skyrocketing costs and the introduction of Health Maintenance Organizations. More and more patients lost their private health insurance and were forced to join an HMO. Doctors of all specialties had to join multiple HMOs or forfeit their practice for lack of patients. And you had to accept the HMO reimbursement schedule, invariably less than what private insurance had paid for the same procedures. At the same time, the cost of medical malpractice insurance continued its yearly rise. When I started as a solo practitioner, my policy cost about $15,000 a year. By 2014, it was over $60,000. It became harder to maintain my office. Supplies, like everything else, were subject to inflation and ate up more and more of my budget. My employees expected yearly raises if they were to stay on the job. I was in a financial crunch.

To add insult to injury, the federal government decreed that all medical records must be in an electronic format. The cost of conversion from paper to computer was typically $75,000. I didn't have that kind of money. Further, the government never established a standard for electronic records. Consequently, although a doctor could share his data with a hospital using the same system, it was useless for any physician or facility using a different one. And, in my opinion, it irreparably harmed the practice of medicine. The computer, not the patient, became the focus of the doctor's attention.

I continued to practice as I always had. I talked with my patients, listened to their concerns, and made mental notes as I did their exams. When done, I dictated my thoughts into a hand-held recorder. My dictation was transcribed onto paper and put in the patient's chart. Today, doctors stare at a computer screen and fill in the blanks as they ask a series of canned questions. They have to even if they don't want to, because that's what the system demands. Leave something blank and you don't get paid. All the humanity has been stripped from my profession.

At age 66, my income wasn't a fifth of what it had been years earlier. My local hospital was taken over by a conglomerate that operated on a for-profit basis. They began to dictate how participating doctors could practice — what procedures they were allowed to perform and what medicines they could prescribe. It was more than I could bear. It was time to quit.

I miss the interaction with my patients. I miss the thrill of a happy delivery. I miss the pleased expression on a patient's face when I have dealt with their problem. But I love being retired. I had never been one to devote my entire life to medicine. I stayed up to date, of course, by reading journals and attending medical meetings. At the same time, I enjoyed a lot of different activities.

In the late '80s, I joined a fencing club and learned to pilot a small plane. When home computers became available, I taught myself to program video games. I spent years learning to play the violin, quite poorly, and had even less success with keyboard, classical, and electric guitars. Target shooting with pistols and rifles had been a hobby since a medical school classmate, Bob Fraker, introduced me to the sport in 1973; and now I have a federal license to manufacture firearms. My small startup business to build custom rifles was, unfortunately, a failure, but I took several of those rifles on big game hunts across the United States and in South Africa.

Most recently, I have taken up building wooden models of warships from the time of Nelson and Napoleon. And books! For years, I collected antique medical books and English histories, some dating back to the 17th century. I continue to read fiction and non-fiction every day, and, like Katie, I never leave the house without a book in case I am delayed.

Life has been, in large part, very kind to me. I spent the first two-thirds learning and practicing a medical career. That's over now, but I feel certain that the future holds many new avenues for me to explore.

Appendix A

MEDICAL TERMINOLOGY

Adenomyosis – A benign but painful disease whereby the endometrium grows within the uterine muscle.

Ambu bag – A facemask and air bag used to ventilate a patient with difficulty breathing.

Analgesic – A medicine, usually taken orally, to relieve pain.

Antepartum – That time in pregnancy before delivery.

Benign – Without life-threatening potential.

Betadine – A form of liquid iodine used to sterilize the skin.

Bilateral Salpingo-Oophorectomy – An operation to remove both Fallopian tubes and ovaries.

Breech Presentation – The fetus lies in the uterus bottom-down (instead of head down).

CA125 – A marker in the blood stream usually elevated in the presence of ovarian cancer.

Carcinoma in situ – Cancer of the cervix confined to the surface layer only and not itself life-threatening.

Cauterize – Burn tissue with chemicals, electricity, or laser.

Cervical Conization – An operation for cervical dysplasia whereby a cone-shaped plug of tissue is removed from the cervix.

Cervical Dysplasia – A change in the epithelium covering the cervix ranging from mild to severe, but not cancer.

Chemotherapy – The treatment of cancer using toxic medicines.

"Circs" – Medical student slang for circumcisions.

Cirrhosis – Damage to the liver causing it to not function properly; often caused by excessive use of alcohol.

Clomid – A medicine taken orally, which forces the ovaries to release an egg.

Colposcopy – A procedure to examine the cervix using a form of binoculars with short focal length and to take samples of any abnormal-appearing tissue.

Cryotherapy – Kill abnormal tissue by freezing, usually using a probe chilled by evaporation of high-pressure gas.

D&C specimen – Tissue scraped from inside the uterus in a procedure known as Dilatation and Curettage.

Debulking – Surgical removal of a large portion of cancer in order for other treatments (radiation, chemotherapy) to be more effective.

Doptone – A hand-held device that uses ultrasound waves to measure fetal heart rate.

Eclampsia – A severe disease of late pregnancy characterized by convulsions, high blood pressure, and proteinuria.

Ectopic mass – A collection of pregnancy tissue and fluid located outside the uterine cavity, typically within the Fallopian tube.

Ectopic pregnancy – A pregnancy growing outside the uterus, usually within the Fallopian tube.

Endometriosis – A benign but painful disease whereby the lining of the uterus (the endometrium) grows within the abdominal cavity.

Episiotomy – An incision in the perineum, either vertical or lateral, made at time of delivery to enlarge the vaginal opening and prevent tearing.

Epithelium – The outermost layer of tissue covering an organ.

Erb's palsy – A partial or complete paralysis of an arm resulting from tearing the nerves in the armpit.

Fetal monitor – A machine that measures and records both uterine contractions and fetal heart rate.

Fibroids – Benign balls of connective tissue that form within the muscle of the uterus.

Folie à Deux – A form of schizophrenia in which two individuals living together share the same delusion.

Follicular cyst – A cyst on the ovary containing a ripening egg which forms in the first two weeks of the menstrual cycle.

Frozen section – A quick way to examine tissues during surgery. The pathologist freezes the specimen to harden it, cuts thin sections with a microtome, stains them, and examines them under a microscope.

Functional Cyst – Ovarian cysts that develop in the normal function of the ovary:; follicular and luteal cysts.

Fundus – The top of the uterus.

Glans –The head of the penis.

Gomco instrument – An instrument utilizing a metal bell and clamp to perform circumcisions.

Human Chorionic Gonadotropin (HCG) – A hormone released by the growing embryo in the early stages of pregnancy.

Hypochondriac – An individual abnormally and unnecessarily concerned about their health.

Hysterectomy – The surgical removal of the uterus.

Hysterosalpingogram (HSG) – An X-ray used to determine the patency of the Fallopian tubes whereby radiopaque dye is injected into the uterus and the tubes observed with a fluoroscope.

Hysteroscope – A telescope the diameter of a soda straw introduced through the cervix to observe the uterine cavity.

Internal podalic version – Turning a fetus within the uterus from breech to vertex by grasping the legs; now obsolete.

Intracranial hemorrhage – Bleeding within the skull, often with bleeding within the brain.

In-vitro fertilization (IVF) – The formation of an embryo by mixing sperm and egg in the laboratory and then implanting the growing embryo in the uterus.

Kisselbach's Area – An area within the nasal septum where arteries join to form a complex.

L&D – Universal slang for "Labor and Delivery."

Laparoscopic – Surgery performed with a laparoscope.

Laparoscopy – To inspect inside a body cavity (in Gynecology, the pelvis) by introducing a telescope through a small incision.

Laparotomy – Any surgical procedure involving a large incision to gain access to the abdominal cavity.

Luteal cyst – A cyst on the ovary formed by the transformation of a follicular cyst after ovulation has occurred.

Malignant – Life-threatening and commonly referred to with cancer.

Mayo stand – A stand at the foot of the operating table on which the scrub nurse arranges her instruments.

McRoberts maneuver – A procedure used to relieve shoulder dystocia whereby an assistant applies pressure just above the mother's pubic arch, allowing the fetal head to slip out.

Medical College Aptitude Test (MCAT) – A standardized test taken by undergraduates in their senior year to determine suitability for medical school.

Methotrexate – A chemotherapeutic agent originally used against cancer.

Mittelschmertz – Originally a German term, now widely used to denote the pain a woman feels when a follicular cyst ruptures and releases an egg; literally "pain in the middle" [of her cycle].

Mohel – A Jew trained in the "covenant of circumcision."

MRI – Magnetic Resonance Imaging, which uses magnetic fields to form images of organs similar to CT scans.

Multigravida – A woman pregnant for the second or succeeding times.

Neonatologist – A physician trained in the pediatric subspecialty of newborn care.

Neoplastic cysts – Ovarian cysts not of a functional nature which may be benign or malignant; literally "new growth" cysts.

Oncologist – A physician who specializes in the treatment of cancer.

Perineum – The area between the vagina and anus.

Peritonitis – Infection of the lining of the abdominal cavity, the peritoneum.

Pitocin – Widely-used trade name for oxytocin, a hormone that stimulates uterine contractions.

Placenta previa – A critical condition of late pregnancy whereby the placenta implants over the opening to the cervix.

Pomeroy Tubal Ligation – A form of female sterilization whereby the Fallopian tubes are gathered into a loop, tied, and a portion of the loop excised.

Primigravida – A woman pregnant for the first time.

Progesterone – A hormone essential to the maintenance of pregnancy; initially produced by a luteal cyst and later by the placenta.

Prolapsed cord – A critical condition of late pregnancy whereby with the rupture of the bag of waters, the umbilical cord drops down between the cervix and the fetal head.

Prolixin – An anti-schizo-phrenic drug which, when given by injection, may be effective for as long as four weeks.

Proteinuria – The presence of abnormal amounts of protein in the urine.

Pulmonologist – A physician trained in the Internal Medicine subspecialty of lung disease.

Salpingostomy – An operation to remove a blockage, typically an ectopic pregnancy, by incising the tube but not removing it. The procedure may be performed either by laparoscopy or laparotomy.

Schadenfreude – A German word meaning "taking pleasure in the misfortune of others."

"Scut work" – Medical student slang for minor tasks beneath the dignity of the resident staff, such as starting IV's and drawing blood.

Shoulder dystocia – A critical condition occurring at delivery whereby the fetal shoulders are too big to fit through the bony pelvic outlet.

"Snow Whited" – Medical student slang for leaving an operating room with gloves untouched by blood, as white as snow.

Stellazine – A major antipsychotic drug in the same family as Thorazine, but not as sedating.

"Studs" – Residents' slang for medical students.

Suprapubic pressure – A maneuver used to relieve shoulder dystocia be applying pressure above the pubic arch; see "McRoberts maneuver."

Talwin – A synthetic narcotic painkiller, sometimes employed in the 1970s instead of morphine, but rarely used today.

Thoracentesis – Tapping fluid accumulated in the chest cavity between the lungs and chest wall.

Thorazine – A major anti-psychotic drug associated with a number of undesirable side effects, including excessive sedation.

Umbilicus – The navel; the "belly button."

Vertex – In this book's context, the fetal head, as in "vertex presentation."

Woods' screw – A maneuver to relieve shoulder dystocia by turning the fetus in a screw-like fashion.

Zavanelli maneuver – A last-ditch maneuver to relieve shoulder dystocia by forcing the fetal head back into the vagina and rushing to Caesarean section.

Appendix B

TOBACCONIST TERMS

Briar – A dense wood made from the roots of Mediterranean trees; considered the best wood for pipes.

Burley – A rather bland tobacco largely grown in Kentucky, usually in cubed form, it forms the basis, if not the entirety, of most common American blends, such as Prince Albert.

Balkan blend – A style that originated with the trademarked "Balkan Sobranie;" it is similar to an English blend but much heavier in Latakia.

English blend – A style favored by discriminating experienced pipe smokers; it is popular both in England and America. Recipes vary, but usually consist of Virginia Bright, Latakia, and Perique.

Exclusive Blends – Produced and sold in vacuum-sealed, four-ounce tins by companies such as Dunhill; they are of the highest quality with prices to match.

Latakia – A pitch-black tobacco originally from Syria; it lends a distinctive smoky smell and flavor to English and Balkan blends.

Meerschaum – A porous mineral from Turkey, carved into very light and cool smoking pipes.

Perique – A tobacco from Louisiana, it is fermented to a moist, purplish-brown color and used to add piquancy to a blend.

Turkish – Grown around the Mediterranean, not just in Turkey; it is cut in strips and adds a unique taste and aroma to English and Balkan-style blends.

Virginia Bright – Originally grown in Virginia and the first tobacco produced by English colonists; it is now grown in several other states. It is used in flake form as a mild basis of many blends.

About the Author

Douglas Edwin Heritage was born in New Jersey in 1948. He majored in pre-medicine at the University of Maryland, College Park, where he graduated in 1971 with High Honors and High Honors in Zoology. He was accepted at the Medical College of Virginia-Virginia Commonwealth University, which he attended from 1971 to 1975, graduating as a Doctor of Medicine.

From 1975 through 1978, Heritage was a resident in the Obstetrics and Gynecology program at the Medical College of Virginia Hospitals. After finishing his residency, he practiced for one year with an established OBG group in Petersburg, Virginia. He left in 1979 to begin solo practice in Woodbridge, Virginia, where he practiced both obstetrics and gynecology until retirement in January of 2014.

Heritage was board certified by the American Board of Obstetrics and Gynecology in 1980 and made a Fellow of the American College of Obstetricians and Gynecologists in 1981. During his time in practice, he received numerous awards from the American Medical Association, the Medical Society of Virginia, and the American College of Obstetricians and Gynecologists.

Dr. Heritage has been happily married to his wife, Katie, for 30 years. They reside in Prince William County, Virginia. He has one grown daughter, Barbara, who lives in Charlottesville, Virginia.

Index

-A-

Adenomyosis, 293, 195, 196
Ambu bag, 293, 222
Analgesic, 293, 247
Antepartum, 293, 232

-B-

Betadine, 293, 158, 221

-C-

CA125, 294, 248, 282, 283
Carcinoma in situ, 294, 274
Cauterize, 294
Cervical Conization, 294, 274

Cervical Dysplasia, 294, 274
Clomid, 294, 225
Cryotherapy, 294, 274

-D-

Doptone, 295, 261

-E-

Eclampsia, 295, 219, 220, 9
Episiotomy, 295, 183, 240-242
Erb's palsy, 295, 240

-F-

Folie à Deux, 295, 139, 167, 171, 8

-G-

Gomco instrument, 296, 256

-H-

Hysterosalpingogram (HSG), 296

-K-

Kisselbach's Area, 297, 99

-L-

Latakia, 301, 302, 25

-M-

McRoberts maneuver, 297, 299, 240

Meerschaum, 302, 19

Methotrexate, 297, 252, 253

Mittelschmertz, 297, 246

Mohel, 297, 256

-P-

Perique, 301, 302, 25

Peritonitis, 298, 226

Pitocin, 298, 262

Pomeroy Tubal Ligation, 298, 174

Progesterone, 298, 246

-S-

Salpingostomy, 299, 253

Schadenfreude, 299, 83, 164

Suprapubic pressure, 299, 240

-T-

Talwin, 299, 190

Thorazine, 299, 300, 139

-Z-

Zavanelli maneuver, 300, 241